TALES of ELOISE

True Tales to Bring a Smile to Your Heart

and an Honored Seat at the Banquet of Life

To: Bill Joyce,
May you have much laughter
and many smiles in your life!
Eloise Farren
05/20/17

Eloise Aitken Farren

Happy Ever After Publications

Oakland, California

Happy Ever After Publications
An imprint of Rose Press
www.rosepress.com
rosepressbooks@yahoo.com

Editing, Book Production, Typesetting: Naomi Rose
Book Layout © 2017 BookDesignTemplates.com

Tales of Eloise / Eloise Aitken Farren. — 1st ed.
ISBN 978-0-9816278-5-4

"Everybody laughs the same in every language because laughter is a universal connection."

—Jakob Smirnoff

IN LOVING MEMORY

My Husband, Sean Farren, the love of my life, who was the
happiest "Tale" of all.
My loving Parents, for their repeated tales of me and for the love
they gave me.

IN LOVING DEDICATION TO

My Family here in America and in Ireland
and all my Friends, for all of you have so blessed my life.

ACKNOWLEDGMENTS

MY HEARTFELT THANKS TO

My Goddaughter, Jamie Ann Cross, for her support and help in getting my book published, and for being a happy tale in my life by always being there for me.

To my wonderful friends—you know who you are—for your encouragement and for being tenacious in making me buckle down and get my book written.

To Sister June Scherelth, a wonderful Nun and a close friend 63years, for her support of my book.

I would especially want to thank Naomi Rose (Author/Editor/Publisher) for making my dream of having this book published become a reality. If not for her expertise, kindness, encouragement, her suggestions and advice, and her uplifting comments to me, I most likely would have given up on this. I can truly say that Naomi was "The Wind Beneath My Wings."

CONTENTS

INTRODUCTION

Does being able to smile or laugh make you feel a little better—even for a moment, or for the rest of the day? Do you feel, as I do, that with instant media we are bombarded daily with sad or depressing events that can often affect the way we feel? Then on top of this, we may have our own trials, tribulations, and sorrows that we are carrying and could use a little relief from it all? In a way, being able to smile or laugh, if only like a bandage on what we are feeling, can help to make us feel a little happier or even better for a wee moment. And that is a gift.

Throughout my life, even as a child, I always enjoyed making others laugh; and as an adult I still do, and I try to do it as often as I can. I also enjoy very much telling my own personal humorous true stories, and jokes or remarks that bring some laughter into the lives of others.

Now that I am 81 years of age, I would love to leave behind some legacy of humor as part of my mission in life to bring about a smile and, even better, some laughter that will still be carried on long after "Digger O' Dell, the friendly undertaker" lays my remains beneath the sod and then shovels along.

PART I

THE FIRST FIVE YEARS OF MY LIFE

1935 – 1940

In a small western town in Colorado, in the summer of 1935, I came into this world. By all odds I should have left it the very same day; yet it was that inner tenacity, which has always stayed with me, that pulled me through the tough battle for life. At the time of my birth, my parents had been married one year and two months. My mother told me that I was a very willful child. And after reading what I have written of my younger years, I know you too will agree.

Since I was an only child, without any relatives living nearby, my parents only had me to talk about to others. So I grew up hearing over and over again these stories about my infancy and early childhood. That is why I remember them to this very day.

"OH NO, KAY!"

My grandmother on my mother's side one afternoon decided to take me with her to her friend's home, where other women friends would be as well for their monthly get-together—you know, catching up on all the news that each other had to share; all the common chit-chat that comes from such meetings. This time, my grandmother—whom we called "Nonie," as she did not like to be called "grandma" or "grandmother" —thought it would be a good time to let the ladies see her wee one, whom they had not met as yet.

The Italian/French custom was that they would have a small glass of wine while they visited with each other. The coffee table was placed so that they all could put their wine glasses on the table as they were visiting. Evidently, the conversation was very intriguing and interesting, as no one was paying attention to me, who had just learned how to walk. And without their knowing it, I very nicely went around the coffee table and drank the wine in the glasses.

Needless to say, they all were horrified when they saw what I had done. My grandmother picked me up and decided that she had better hurry and bring me home. When she arrived at the house, she knocked on the door; and when my dad opened the door, my grandmother—not saying a word—handed me to my father, and turned around and quickly left.

My father carried me into the bedroom and placed me on

their bed to change my wet diapers. As he was getting a clean diaper, he heard a thump—and there I was on the floor. Instead of crying I was laughing in bewilderment. Because of my actions, he picked me up, and smelt my breath, and yelled to my mom, "Oh no, Kay, she's drunk!"

I never had any bad effects from the wine, and my understanding is that my grandmother never took me with her again until I was much older.

ME AND MY SHOES

Here are several tales about me and my shoes.

Tale # 1: "Let *Me* Do It!"

I was a very strong-willed baby, and this really showed up when it came to my wearing shoes. I did not like to wear shoes. And even to this day, when I come home the first thing I do is to take off my shoes.

This one afternoon, my Dad's Irish mom, who was a very proper and dignified lady, came for a short visit. By the way, at first she resented my Dad marrying an Italian/French Catholic, and so just tolerated my mother in the beginning of their marriage. During her visit, my parents mentioned to her that they couldn't keep shoes on my feet, and she replied, "Nonsense, you just don't know how to tie them properly so she can't take them off. Here, *I* will do it and show you that there will be no way that baby is going to take off her shoes."

My parents let my grandmother have her way, so she proceeded to tie my shoes and put me back in my crib with a smile of satisfaction on her face, knowing that she had taken care of the problem. When it came time for her to leave, she looked at me, who was still awake and playing in my crib.

As she looked into the crib, she saw the shoes lying by

themselves and not on my feet. My grandmother was so shocked that all she could say was, "Well, I never!" And with a red face, out the door she went without saying another word, and left my parents smiling at each other.

Tale # 2: "Kay, What Happened to the Shoe?"

One day, my father decided he wanted to help my mother by getting me dressed for the day. When he went to put on my shoes, he could only find one shoe. My mother, hearing my father yell, "I can't find her other shoe!" and noting a touch of irritation in his voice, decided she had better help in finding the shoe.

The search ended up in a dismal failure. Nowhere could that shoe be found. In frustration, my father said to my mom, "Kay, I can't understand how one shoe can be missing like this!" He then said, "Shoes just don't disappear into thin air." My poor mother was beside herself, as she had not a clue as to what happened to that shoe and also felt that my dad was holding her responsible for the missing shoe. The truth behind my dad's frustration was that my parents were poor, and my dad was wondering where he was going to get the money to buy me another pair of shoes. Times were hard, as everyone was still suffering the effects from the Great Depression and money was hard to come by, even to buy baby shoes.

The lost shoe was never found—until one day, months later, my father was in the basement of our home, scooping up coal with a shovel from the coal bin to put into the bucket that would be placed next to the kitchen stove and used for fuel for the fire. As my father took another scoop of the coal, what do you think he saw there, lying in the coal bin? Yes, you've guessed it—the lost tan shoe, all black from coal dust after being there for months in the coal bin. Where I had, for some reason— only heaven knows why—decided to throw the one shoe down the coal chute, through a small door on the outside of the house where the delivery men would deliver the coal down the chute into the basement coal room. Knowing me, it was a miracle that I never tried going down the coal chute myself!

Tale #3: Another Shoe Story

Yes, once again! This time, not only was *one* shoe lost but also *both* shoes were missing.

In the thirties, it was not unusual for some homes not to have grass in their yards, nor a cement sidewalk. Usually, it could be a wooden walk or flat stone walkway. When it would rain, the yard could become very muddy and stay that way for a couple of days.

The yard was fenced in, and so it was safe to let me out in the yard to play. This one day after a good rainstorm, my mother let me outside to play. She would check on me from the window ever so often to be sure I was okay, as I was only four years of age at that time.

When my mother called me to come in, she didn't really notice me at first and so didn't see that I was not wearing any shoes. When she finally took notice, she wasn't concerned about me not having my shoes on, for when I was in the house I would often manage to get my shoes off. As you well remember, I did not like wearing shoes. However, the next morning was a different story: when she went to put my shoes on, she couldn't find them anywhere. And to make matters even worse, I only had the one pair, as we were quite poor at the time and my parents could only afford to buy me one pair of shoes at a time.

My mom looked all over in the house and even out in the yard—no shoes. She just could not figure out why she could not find them, and she could not get an answer out of me, as well; for every time she asked me, all she got was a shrug of my shoulders that meant "I don't know." Finally, after some time, she finally gave up looking, as to her it seemed to be a lost cause. Not only that—she was not very happy about telling my dad that my shoes were missing again, as always, as if it was her fault.

My parents had given up hope of ever finding my shoes, until a couple of days later, the ground outside had dried up after the heavy rainstorm. And where the mud puddle once was, there, in the middle of the dried-up puddle, was a pair of shoes stuck in the mud. Where I had walked out of them.

FROM THE MOUTH OF A BABE

I could walk before I talked very much—just a couple of words, like "mama" or "papa." My parents were fearful that I had something wrong with me, as I should by now be talking.

It was not long after this story I am now telling that I really startled my mother. She was busy putting away the pans in the cupboard after washing dishes. And all of a sudden she heard a deep voice saying. "You better sit down or you will fall down." She almost dropped the pans she was holding! She turned, and there I was, standing in my highchair, repeating what *she* would say to me when I would stand up in my highchair. From that day on, they found out that I could talk using sentences. And why I didn't do this earlier, they didn't have a clue.

As I tell others today, that was the first sentence out of my mouth, and I've never stopped talking since.

WHAT, NO COFFEE?

One Sunday afternoon, my parents and I were at my grandmother's home, visiting. My parents were seated at the kitchen table, and I was sitting in a highchair that my grandmother had kept for her grandchildren. As always, when someone would come to visit, my grandmother would offer something to drink.

It happened on this day that my parents wanted coffee, so my grandmother filled their cups with coffee and gave me a glass of milk. I started fussing, as I didn't want milk—*I* wanted to have coffee, too. My father tried to get me to drink my milk by using different antics, but all failed. So then he whispered in my grandmother's ear to take my milk and secretly put it into a coffee cup, and then he said to her, "She won't know the difference."

My grandmother put the milk in the cup and then placed it in front of me on my high chair. I took the cup in my hands and peered inside the cup. Then my eyes flashed in anger as I shouted out, "Doggone it, I wanted cha-chi!"

PART II

TALES BETWEEN 3 AND 5 YEARS OF AGE

WHAT IN THE WORLD??

This was another story I heard my mom telling family and friends. Really, I do not know how old I was at this time.

My mother was out in the backyard hanging up clothes on the line when she heard water running in the kitchen. Thinking that a pipe was broken, she rushed into the house and into the kitchen—and there was the water, running full blast from the faucets in the sink and spilling over on to the floor.

I was standing over in the corner, where I had punished myself. (Standing in the corner was the way I would be punished if I did something I should not do.) I had climbed up on the wooden chair in front of the sink and turned on the faucets, and then I didn't know how to turn them off. So, knowing that I must have done something really bad, I cornered myself.

OH, THAT NAUGHTY BIRD

My mother was inside the house doing dishes when she heard me outside in the back yard, yelling in an angry voice. My mother hurried outside to see who I was yelling at—and to her surprise, there was not a soul around except for a bird sitting on the fence.

She noticed that I was yelling at the bird, which seemed to be completely ignoring me, and she said, "Eloise, why are you yelling at the poor little bird?"

I spoke up and said, "I'm bawling out this naughty bird for always telling on me."

My mother paused for a moment and then started laughing to herself as she realized the reason for my yelling at the bird.

When I would be doing something I shouldn't be doing and my mother would catch me without my knowing it, she would then get after me for my misdeeds. I just couldn't understand how in the world she could know when I was doing something wrong. So I would ask her, "Mama how did you find out?"

And she would always say to me: "I found out because a little bird told me."

THE NURSERY SCHOOL

Looking back on my nursery-school days (I believe I was four years of age at the time), believe it or not, I can remember even to this day my experience there. That memory has never left me.

At lunchtime I had to sit at little table by myself, behind a portable wooden divider. And yes, I do remember why. Before the children could eat their lunch, they would have to take a teaspoon of cod-liver oil; and after my first taste of that horrible, awful stuff, I made up my mind that was it! I wanted no more!

I can still see, today, this (to me) huge woman trying to get me to take the cod-liver oil. Not only did she work to pry my mouth open, but also after that awful stuff was in my mouth, I spit it out! Seeing that I was so stubborn, the only alternative for her was to put me behind the wooden portable divider, where I would not be a bad example to the other children by not taking my cod-liver oil.

Not only do I remember this room, with its tables and chairs, toys, books, and so on, I also remember the other room. It had small beds with rollers. You may wonder why I mentioned rollers on the bed. The reason is that I wouldn't take my afternoon naps, either (I always hated taking naps—even to this day, at 81 years of age, I still do not take naps except when I am sick and bedridden), so the teacher would roll my bed, with me on it, into the cloak room to stay there during nap time. I can still see the coats hanging from the hooks on the wall on either side of my bed.

Looking back on my nursery days, I am sure the teachers really dreaded seeing me coming in the door (as I am sure I was a handful)—and celebrated the day when I left for good.

"KAY, WHAT DID YOU DO?"

Now, I must begin this story by mentioning two important factors:

One: on my father's side of the family, there is a long tradition of proud Scotsmen who were the Sept of the Clan MacDonald, and our particular ancestors were, among other things, hereditary pipers of the Clan MacDonald, long remaining loyal to the exiled Stuarts who tried to restore the house of Stuart to the Throne.

It was during this time that our ancestor Malcolm Darroch and our forefathers joined the gathering of the other Highland Clansmen to fight with their leader, Charles Edward Stuart, commonly known as Bonnie Prince Charlie, against the English. This was called the Jacobite Uprising, in 1745, which ended in disaster and the final defeat of the Jacobite cause at the battle of Culloden Moor in Scotland. Bonnie Prince Charlie, with a price on his head, sailed to France; and Malcolm Darroch, with his clan having a price on their head, fled from the Highlands down to the Lowlands. There, he took refuge with relatives by the name of Aitken and changed his name to Malcolm Aitken, and James Darroch changed his name to James Aitken.

In 1785, James and Robert Aitken became Burgesses of Glasgow, Scotland. My great-grandfather, who was the son of Robert Aitken, came to America in 1842, worked on the River

Boats on the Mississippi River, and, hearing about gold in California, came there by sea, sailing to Panama and from there to San Francisco in 1849. From there, he sailed up the river to Sacramento, and from there to Jackson, California; and years later he came to Oakland, California. This is where my grandfather, William Aitken, grew up. William went to Oakland Tech, then graduated from Cal University, and from there went to Colorado Springs, Colorado, where my father, Raymond, was born in 1899. Sometime in the 1920s, my grandfather and his family moved to Durango, Colorado. And that is where my father married my mother, Catherine Fiorini, in 1934, and where I was born in 1935.

Two: My mother—who was Italian and French and, horrors! a Catholic—married my father against the wishes of his mother, Anna Quinn (who was Protestant Irish) and his father (the proud Scotsman, William Aitken, who was also Protestant). It really was my father's mother who disliked the Catholics; my grandfather had a more open view in this matter, as he was accepting of all religions.

I know you are asking, "What has this do with your story?" It is important that you know this background in order for the rest of my story to make sense.

It was wintertime, and my mother felt that I should have a better head covering for when I was outside in the cold weather. I was four years old, and we did not have a car, which meant we would do a lot of walking.

My mother felt that she needed to have something really warm for my head. And as she was thinking about this, she remembered the lovely wool plaid material that my father kept neatly folded in his dresser drawer. My mother—having not a clue or knowledge of the significance of this lovely plaid material that lay in the drawer year after year—thought to herself, "What a shame that this is not being put to some good use!" And so she decided, "This lovely material would make a wonderful parka." (A head covering, often having a peak that completely covers your head and the back of your neck, the material being tied in the front.)

So my mother went to work, and cut up the lovely plaid material and sewed it together, making a very nice, comfy parka for her darling little girl. She was so proud of her efforts, as she looked at me wearing my parka, that she just could not keep this beautiful workmanship to herself. So she decided to take me to my father's parents to show off her masterpiece.

Well, the moment she entered my grandparents' house, she brought me over to the smoking chair where my grandfather was sitting and said to him: "Look at the parka I made for Eloise from the material I found in Raymond's drawer."

My grandfather recognized the plaid material that was now on top of my head; and instead of expressing adulation over the parka, he became exceedingly upset with my mother; and in a livid, stern voice, he said to her, "Kay, I want you to leave this house right now!"

My mother left with me in a hurry out the door, and couldn't understand why my grandfather was so very angry with her. It wasn't long after until my father came home from work and found my mom still crying: not only about my grandfather being angry with her, but also with disappointment that he hadn't appreciated the lovely parka she had made for me.

After my father calmed her down, he explained to her what she had done—that she had cut up an ancient family plaid heirloom, the Royal Tartan from the Hereditary Pipers, which had been handed down in the Darroch/Aitken family for generations, from the first-born son and on and on until it was handed down to my father, the first-born son in his generation.

In ending my tale, I will say that my grandfather—after his shock of the desecration of the family heirloom—forgave my mother, and she was welcomed back into the Aitken household. However, her misdeed was never forgotten.

MY MOTHER'S OTHER SEWING ADVENTURE

My mother took me with her one day to visit a dear friend who had twin girls my age. After we had entered the house, my mother's friend noticed the bonnet on my head that my mom had made for me. She was so taken with it that she asked my mother if she could look at it and see how it was made, as she would so much love to make ones just like it for her twins, as well.

My mother at once went over to me to take the bonnet off my head. But when I saw her coming, I put my hands up onto my bonnet and held on so tightly that my mom could not remove it from my head. She could not understand why I was so stubborn in not letting her take it off, and proceeded to tell me that if I didn't take off my bonnet, I would be punished for being so stubborn.

Tears started running down my face as I took off the bonnet. And there, lying on top of my head, were two lollipops that my mom had bought for me. I had hidden them there so that I would not have to share them with the twins, as that would mean I wouldn't have one for myself. I was brought up to never to eat anything in front of anyone if you can't share with them. So with tears still streaming down, I took the lollipops from my head and gave them to the girls.

My mom felt terrible. She had not realized that I had hidden the lollipops under my bonnet, and she would not have made me remove my bonnet if she had.

After we left the house, she made up for it by buying me two more lollipops.

THAT DIRTY STORK

When I was young, in explanation to the question "Where do babies come from?" the answer given was: "The Stork." I remember seeing in books, or even advertisements in magazines, the huge white stork flying in the sky; and in his beak was a diaper or blanket like a bundle; and in this bundle was a baby. The stork was delivering the baby to someone's house.

My mother had a tubule pregnancy, which not only caused her to lose the baby (a boy), but also prevented her from having any other children. This was in the 1930s, when medical procedures were not like they are today.

Being an only child and not having any brother or sisters, I had no knowledge when I was young about the actual way a baby comes into this world. All I knew was that the stork brought the babies. I wanted so badly to have a baby brother or sister that I would go outside and look up into the sky, looking for that stork so I could put my order in for a baby brother or sister, as I was told that was how it was done. The stork was nowhere to be seen.

When I was five years of age, I came running to my mother with a magazine that had a picture of the Dionne Quintuplets when they were babies. They had been born a year before me, in 1934. I can't rightly say how I found the picture of the five infant babies, or if someone had shown it to me. All I remember is hearing my mother talking over the following years about how I came running into the room where she was, and holding the picture right in front of my mother's face. With my finger, I started counting the babies: "1, 2, 3, 4, 5"—and then, with an angry look on my face, I shouted: "That dirty stork brought that woman all those babies, and he didn't even bring us one!" I do remember that from that day on, I had a real dislike for that stork, who never brought me a baby brother or sister.

THOSE DARN MOSQUITOES

When I was five years of age, my mother and I would sometimes go to the train station to meet my father, who was driving the Rio Grande train back home after one of his runs. We would have to cross over a bridge in order to get to the station.

On this one particular day, the mosquitoes were flying around us in droves. Not only were they flying around, but they were trying very hard to use us for their evening meal, as well. We kept swatting and waving our hands around, trying to keep them away or off us. Finally, in disgust, I yelled out: "Mama, I wish God gave these darn mosquitoes ears—I would sure bawl them out." End of tale.

PART III

LIFE IN THE APARTMENT BUILDING
4 TO 5 YEARS OLD

"ELOISE, HOW COULD YOU?"

I really don't know how old I was when we were living in an apartment building. I do know that it was before I was in the first grade. And I do remember very well the apartment.

We lived in a two-room apartment—the kitchen, which also was part of a living room, and the one bedroom. There was only one bathroom in the building, which all the tenants shared. It had a toilet, sink, and bathtub. Tenants were allowed to take a bath only once a week. The rest of the time you washed up in the sink.

I know you are wondering why I am mentioning the bathroom and why I remember it so well. The reason was that I hated taking a bath (though I did love the little sponge turtle that was my washcloth). Because after I was bathed, my mother would then wash my hair, and would put my head under the faucet to rinse it, with the water running full blast. I would always cry out "You're drowning me, you're drowning me!" I found this to be so frightening that I never forgot it.

The building itself was a large two-story building. The grocery store and a laundry/dry cleaner shop were on the ground floor, and on top were the apartments. These did not cover the whole roof, but were set back from the outside walls of the grocery store and laundry. The only entrance into the apartments was by going up wooden stairs in the back alley. The way the apartment building was situated on the second floor over the laundry allowed a space on the roof for a large window, made up of small panes of glass, called a "skylight." This was the source of light for the laundry below.

Yes, I know you are now wondering what is so important about the skylight that I had to write about it. I will tell you why: the skylight always seemed to fascinate me, as it could be seen as you were going up or down the wooden stairs. It wasn't long before I discovered that I could access that part of the roof by stepping off the stairs that were closest to the roof. The way the stairs were built, it was very easy for a girl my age to step off the stairs onto the roof.

And so one day, I did. Without my mother knowing. She definitely would not have approved.

And as I went over to the window, I looked at the small panes of glass—and what possessed me to do this, I cannot tell you (I could say, as on the old Flip Wilson show on TV, "the Devil made me do it!"), but I took my one foot and stamped on the glass and it broke. Oh, it was so much fun that I started stamping on the other panes of glass. The noise of the falling and breaking of glass immediately caught the attention of the laundry staff below. Before I knew it, the owner of the laundry came running out of the downstairs door, yelling at the top of his lungs and heading for the stairs. I started running for the stairs, as well, as I knew I was in big trouble.

My mom, hearing the commotion, came out and was standing on the landing at the top of the stairs when I ran right past her into the hallway and into our apartment.

Naturally, the owner of the building was exceedingly angry. My mother came back into the apartment, and the next thing I knew I was over my mother's knee getting spanked (in those days, spanking was not considered child abuse). The message was received, and I never ventured over that part of the roof again.

"MAMA, I HAVE BOO-BOOS"

While we were still living at the apartment, I would play with a boy who lived in the next apartment from ours.

The Walt Disney movie "Snow White and the Seven Dwarfs" was playing at the one-and-only movie theater in the town. Not only did my mother want to take me to see the movie, she also was looking forward to seeing it herself, as others had told her how wonderful it was and that she should not miss it.

Early one afternoon, my mother gave me a hot bath, got me all dressed up, and then proceeded to get herself ready for going to the movie. As she was getting ready, without her knowing it I went next door to play with the little boy. We had not played together too long when my mother figured out where I was and came to get me, as it was time to go to the movie. When I saw her at the door, I ran over to her and said: "Mama, we didn't have enough iodine to cover all my boo-boos."

My mother took one look at me and saw brownish dots of iodine covering some of the spots that looked like tiny blisters all over my entire body. She realized right away that the hot bath she had given me had brought out to the surface of my body these tiny blisters—which turned out to be chicken pox.

My mother hurried and found the little boy's mother sitting outside on the wooden stairs, and said to her, "If your boy hasn't had the chicken pox, I'm sorry to say he sure is going to get them now. My daughter is covered with them."

Needless to say, we didn't go to the movie. It was years later before I saw "Snow White and the Seven Dwarfs." Yes, I loved that movie—so much so that I bought it on a VCR tape and still have it in my collection, along with other Walt Disney movies.

PART IV

TALES FROM 5 TO 6 YEARS OF AGE

A SMALL TOWN IN COLORADO

When I was five years of age, we moved to a very small town. It was located high up in the Colorado Rockies! The town had only one grocery store, which carried other items as well as food. The town folk needing other supplies would go to a larger town not that far away. The main source of transportation would be what they lovingly called the "Galloping Goose." In fact, my father was the engineer for a while. The Galloping Goose looked like a small bus or shuttle bus. The only difference was that instead of rubber tires, it had wheels—the same as on the Rio Grande train—and would travel on the railroad tracks. It did not ride smoothly like a passenger train; it was a very bumpy ride. And that is why it was called the Galloping Goose.

CHILDREN SHOULD BE SEEN
AND NOT HEARD

When I five years of age, my father, who was an engineer on the Rio Grande Railroad, was invited by his boss to come over this one evening for dinner. My father felt so good about being invited to his home, for this was an exception: his boss was not noted for inviting employees into his home, especially for dinner. And of course, my mom and I were invited to come, as well.

Before we left the house, my father went over some rules that I needed to follow while we were there, and he ended with the admonition, "No interrupting the adults while they are talking. Remain quiet unless they are talking to you." Then he would say this admonition (I so remember this quote, as it came from a poem which I heard many times): "Children should be seen and not heard."

It was important to my father that we all made a good impression, since this was the first time my father's boss and his wife would meet us. After the evening meal, we were taken into the living room. Up to this time, I was well behaved and sitting quietly while my father and his boss were visiting.

On the way to the living room, my father's boss had removed his dentures from his mouth and then proceeded to the living room. As my father's boss was talking, my dad happened to look over at me and saw that I was pulling on my teeth really hard. He kept watching me pulling away at my teeth and wondering what in the world I was doing. Finally, he could not stand it any longer and asked me, "Eloise, why are you tugging at your teeth? Do they hurt?" And I replied: "Oh no, daddy, I'm just trying to take out my teeth so that I can talk like Mr. Lyons."

My understanding is that my father was very embarrassed by what I had said. He did not know his boss well enough to know how he would take this comment from me. In my father's mind, I am sure he said, "No words could be truer than 'Children should be seen and not heard.'"

THE GROCERY-MAN'S DAUGHTER

It was at this time, when I was in the first grade, that my best friend was the Grocery-man's daughter. (We called him "the Grocery-man," as he owned the one and only grocery store.) His daughter and I would play together all the time—until one fateful day when her father came to our home and would not allow me to play with his daughter any more.

On this day, after my friend had gone back home from playing with me, her father came to our house very upset and angry. My father answered the door and invited the Grocery-man to come in—which he didn't. He just stood there on the porch and in a loud voice said to my father, "I don't want your daughter to play with my girl anymore!" My father asked him why, and what had I done that made him so upset? He replied, "Never mind what she has done. All I am saying is, I don't want her around my daughter anymore!" Again, my father said, "I wish you would tell me why." The Grocery-man answered, "She is a bad example for my daughter, and that's it!" He turned and left my father standing in the doorway, wondering what it was I had done that so upset the Grocery-man!

Then my father came to me and asked, "What did you do to make your friend's father so upset that he doesn't want you to play with his daughter anymore?" I said, "I didn't do anything, daddy." My dad replied, "You must have done something.

Now think: what did you do?" I replied again, "Daddy, really, I didn't do anything. I only taught her a song that I learned from you singing it all the time." (My father was great for making up songs; and actually, some of them were pretty good.) My father asked me what song was that; he had never ever thought of me memorizing any of his songs.

So I started singing to him: "Fly, fly, flew through the door. Flew through the door of the Grocery Store, pooped on the sugar and pooped on the ham and didn't give a damn for the Grocery-man."

OH, THOSE DELICIOUS DONUTS

My dear father always loved to cook. One day he was hungry for donuts, and so he decided to make some. And when he had finished, he put the donuts in a small enamel roasting pan that had a lid on it. Then he asked my mom if she would like to go with him to get his paycheck at the train depot. Since ours was a small town, it was safe to leave me at home. And besides, it wasn't that far for them to go. They would be back home in no time.

Well, as my parents were coming back from the train depot, they happened to notice some kids with donuts in their hands. My father said to my mom, "Gee, Kay, it looks like *everyone's* decided to make donuts today."

When they got back home, I was playing house outside with a couple of my friends. My mother turned to the task of getting supper ready, as it was getting around that time. My father said to her, "Kay, don't cook very much, so that we will have room in our stomachs for all the donuts that I made today."

When we had finished eating our small meal, my father got up and picked up the pan that held the donuts. And as he was bringing the covered roasting pan to the table, he said, "I have been so looking forward to having these donuts—I can hardly wait." So saying, he set the pan down on the middle of the kitchen table where we were still sitting, and took the lid off.

But when he looked inside, a painful look came over his face. Instead of the many donuts he was looking forward to, there were just three left on the bottom of the pan.

"Eloise," he questioned me, "what happened to all my donuts?"

"Well, Daddy," I said, "I saved one for each of us. You always tell me that I should share, and that is what I did. I went out and got my friends to come over and get some."

MY FIRST TIME SEEING SANTA CLAUS

It was getting close to Christmas, so my mother took me with her to do her Christmas shopping. This was my very first time in this city, and I was so in awe of the Christmas lights and decorations on the outside streets, and in all the stores, as well. It was all was so wonderful and magical to me. I still can remember seeing that awesome sight even to this very day. In fact, I remember everything about this trip to the city. It actually was my first experience of being in a city.

I needed new shoes, as the shoes on my feet were really worn, so my mother decided that this would be the first thing on her agenda. She took me to the store that carried shoes along with other goods. We went over to the shoe department and found me a pair of shoes that fit me and also was to my liking. I was so happy with my new shoes that I wanted to wear them right away; and my mother let me, as she knew this was such a big thing for me.

I believed in Santa Claus, and there was a live Santa in this store. I wanted to see him and tell him what I wanted him to bring me for Christmas. I was so excited, as my mother and I waited in line. This was my very first time to see Santa Claus in person; before that, I only had seen him in storybooks.

At last my time came; and so I went up and sat on his

lap, and told him all that I wanted for Christmas, and showed him my new shoes. After I was through, he gave me a candy cane, and I happily left the store with my mother, holding her hand.

I was the happiest girl ever—UNTIL we went into another store, and as we walked into the store, here was Santa! He had gotten to the store before I did, and here he was, coming toward me. As he stooped over to talk with me, he asked me, "Little Girl, what would you like Santa to bring you for Christmas?"

Oh no—how terrible, how very terrible! Santa had forgotten what I had told him already in the other store. So I said to him, "Don't you remember? I told you already!" Santa said; "Oh yes, better tell me again!" And so I did. And as he walked away, I started to cry and said to my mother, "Mama, what if Santa doesn't remember? What if he forgets again? He won't bring me my toys." My mother tried to reassure me that Santa wouldn't forget this time, for sure, and not to worry.

But I did worry, clear up to Christmas Day. Even when I was put to bed that Christmas Eve night, I said to my dad, who always tucked me and my panda into bed, "Daddy, are you sure Santa will remember what to bring me?" My father reassured me, and told me to not get up out of bed in the morning until I heard the bell ring. Then, I could go and see what Santa had brought me.

I remember jumping out of bed when I heard the bell (to

this day I don't know what was used to sound like a bell, as to my knowledge we didn't have one). And when I walked into the living room, here was a Christmas tree that Santa had brought me. It was my very first Christmas tree, and it was the most beautiful tree, with ornaments and real lit candles (not lights) attached to the branches that turned the room into a wonderland.

And underneath the tree were the toys I had asked Santa to bring me. Santa had *not* forgotten. I was so happy! Santa even brought me more than I had asked for, as under the tree in a box were puppies, and they were alive! I was so excited and thrilled. How did Santa know that I loved puppies?

I never knew that the stray dog my parents took in was going to have puppies. And when she was due, they put her in the spare room of our house and kept her there until Christmas Day. I have always treasured that Christmas, even to this day.

PART V

TALES FROM GRADE-SCHOOL YEARS: 2^(ND) – 6^(TH) GRADE

INTRODUCTION TO THE TALES: 1941 - 1949

In 1941, we moved to a small railroad and farming town on the desert. My father first was an engineer on the Rio Grande Railroad in Colorado. From there, he changed to the Union Pacific Railroad, which created our move to a small town that was the central stopping-place for trains between one state and another.

The town was made up of a General Store, a Gas Station, a small four-room School, a Town Hall, one Church, a small Movie Theater, a Beanery (Cafe), the Train Depot, an Ice House, and a Post Office.

The Post Office

The Post Office consisted of one large room partitioned into two parts: one where people would come in to pick up the mail, and the other where the Postmistress lived (behind the partition that extended from one wall to the other). There was also a large window in the center of this partition that would open up by pushing up a wooden panel. A large counter under the window opening extended on both sides, where people could pick up their packages that were in the Postmistress's quarters or sign documents, etc. When the window was open, you would see a wooden table with a couple of chairs, a cupboard for her dishes, etc., and a large potbelly stove with a teakettle on it, with steam pouring out of the spout.

I will now share with you why I mentioned the steaming teakettle on the stove in the Post Office. Not only did the Postmistress use the kettle for tea and so on; she would also use the steam from the teakettle to open personal letters sent in the mail, and then glue them back up again. In this way, she found out a lot about the people in the community.

Now you may ask, "How do you know this to be true?" as the Postmistress certainly would not steam open private letters when others were around. So I will tell you.

One day, my mother went to the Post Office to pick up her mail and also have a wee chat with the Postmistress. My mom then went to her mailbox and took out her mail. There was a letter from her mother in Colorado, from whom she had not heard from in a long time. My mother was very happy to see the letter from her mom, as she had been worried about her and was hoping everything was okay.

With the mail in her hand, my mother turned to leave. And as she was going out the
Door, the Postmistress yelled to her, "Have fun with your mom and brothers when they come next week to see you." My mom wondered how in the world would she know something like that? For sure, she herself didn't know anything about their coming.

There is an expression that was often used: "Letting the cat out of the bag," meaning when a person would tell something they were not supposed to tell. The Postmistress certainly did let the cat out of the bag; for when my mom got home, she opened the letter from my grandmother telling my mom that she and my mom's three brothers were coming to spend a week with us the following week So now my mom knew that the only way the Postmistress could have known that they were coming was by steaming open the envelope and reading the letter.

Outdoor Bathrooms

It was an exception for anyone in or outside of town to have an indoor bathroom. The majority of us did not. We had little wooden frame structures outside, a little ways from the house, called an "Outhouse"—a fancy name for toilet. At Halloween time, the older boys loved nothing more than to go through the town turning over the "Outhouses," as most of them were not secured to the wooden flooring. However, the classier ones had cement flooring, which prevented them from being tipped over.

Our outhouse had a door with a latch on the inside to lock it. On the inside of the outhouse was a long narrow bench with one or two large round holes cut in it for you to sit down on when you were going to the bathroom. Underneath the wooden bench where you were sitting was a huge dirt hole in the ground. This structure was our toilet, without lights, heat, or water. For most people, the toilet paper was pages from the Sears Catalog, or magazines that would be torn off sheet by sheet. Now, using this type of toilet paper was not a bit bad, for you could also read or look at pictures from them while you were sitting. We were recycling the newspapers and magazines without ever realizing it.

Those of us who did not have indoor plumbing (except for the kitchen sink, which had only cold water in the faucet) would bathe in the kitchen, using a large round metal tub for our bathtub. In the wintertime, we would bathe right next to the wooden/coal stove to keep us warm. We would use the running cold water in the kitchen sink for our daily ablutions. One of the greatest thrills for me was when we were on vacation and we would stay in a hotel or at my grandmother's with "real indoor bathrooms"! I could hardly wait to take a bath in a real tub. I would soak in the tub for such a long time that my mother finally would yell at me to get out of the tub so others could use the bathroom.

The Railroad

The Railroad was the main hub of the community, which was known as "Railroad Town." The Railroad had a rooming house for the Railroad men. They did not live there full-time but would stay overnight (or even longer) while they waited to take their assigned train out to its destination.

The Movie Theater

The town could also boast of its Movie Theater, which showed a movie every Saturday night. The man who owned it would run the movies, as well. It was not unusual for the loudspeaker to come on during the movie and call out the name of a Railroad man, telling him that his train was ready to be taken out of town. Then the movie would start again. These days, our movies have commercials.

The Beanery

The Railroad owned the one-and-only restaurant, called the Beanery, which was located on the same platform as the train depot, so that the men working in the railroad yards or staying in town between runs (that is, from one work destination to the other) would have a place to eat. The restaurant was also open for the townspeople and travelers, as well.

The Ice House

The Ice House was the size of a barn, and was right next to the Beanery. It got its name because that was where huge, square blocks of ice were kept in sawdust. They were kept frozen by what they called "hot ice," which also were in blocks but were made of a chemical to keep the ice from melting. The blocks of ice were used for the passenger trains that would stop at the station—for the drinking fountains at the end of each car, for the cooks in the kitchen, and for the lounge where alcoholic drinks were served. The blocks of ice would be brought on the train by workmen, who would carry them using a huge claw-like clamp that fit over the block of ice.

We kids had easy access into the Ice House, as the doors were never locked. However, you would not want to be caught carrying any of the ice outside, as that would be considered stealing. What we loved about the Ice House was how cool it was in the hot summertime (remember, we lived in the desert). It was so much fun to play in there! They had ropes for lifting the ice tied to the beams of the building, and we kids loved to swing from one block of ice onto another block of ice. None of us got hurt if we fell, due to the full soft carpet of sawdust below. When I come to think of it, it is a good thing that people who used the ice didn't know about us standing on top of it with our dirty shoes.

The Newsstand

There was a Newspaper stand, which was between the Depot and the Restaurant. It was a small, square-shaped building, with glass windows on all four sides that could be opened up and latched at the top. It was a lot like the Newsstands in airports today. The only difference was that you could not go inside the stand, as you can in the airport. It had newspapers, magazines, comic books, soda pop, juices, coffee, candy, gum, peanuts, candy popcorn, cigarettes, cigars, tobacco, etc.

It was also a favorite place for us kids, if we had the money. For a time, I had found a great way of my getting money: It was during the Second World War, and the troop trains carrying the soldiers would stop there at the Depot. Some of the soldiers would get off the train, but most would stay on inside and they would look out the open windows of the train. There, they would see a poor-looking orphan standing there very pathetically looking at them—now, that was me—so they would reach into their pockets and throw coins out the window for me. I would hurry and run around, and pick up all the change they had thrown. It was great for me—until the one day when my father was the engineer on the train, and he saw yours truly picking up the money given to me by the soldiers. So all that came to an abrupt end.

Not only did the troop trains stop at our train depot, but the passenger trains would also stop there to have a complete check up for brake oil, etc. (Being a steam engine, it needed to be refilled with water, as well, from the tall, towering wooden water-tank.) The passengers would have time to get off the train and walk around the area to stretch their legs, and also take advantage of purchasing what they would like to have at the Newspaper stand or get a cup of coffee in the Beanery.

The Movie Train

I remember the time when I was 12 years of age (in 1947) and we heard that movie actors, producers, and directors would be on a special train, and it would be stopping at our station. In a small town, it didn't take long for the news to get around; and so a bunch of us kids went down to the station to wait for the train to come in, even though it was arriving way early in the morning, just after sunrise. The movie actors and movie personnel were on their way to Salt Lake City for the premiere of their movie, "Forever Amber," starring Linda Darnell and Cornell Wilde.

We were excited when some of the stars got off the train. However, we girls found that some of our "movie queens" were not quite as beautiful as we had seen them onscreen. They were lacking in make-up, some had tousled hair, and they were still in nightclothes, with robes covering them, to greet all of us adoring young fans. Mind you, being young, we did not take into consideration that it was way early in the morning. Looking back now, I am so very grateful to these stars. More than likely, they would have rather stayed in their warm, cozy berths than be outside with a nip in the air, greeting all of us adoring fans. We had never seen movie stars in person before, and they gave all of us the thrill of a lifetime, which I am sure none of us have ever forgotten.

The Desert and Its Inhabitants

Our town was part of a desert, with cactus, tumbleweeds, sagebrush, sand dunes, etc. There also were all kinds of insects, such as Tarantulas, Black Widow Spiders, Centipedes, Scorpions, and a variety of snakes, including the poisonous Rattle Snake and the Blue Mountain Racer. We also had the Blow Snake, which derived its name from the fact that, when it felt threatened, it would puff up, making a blowing sound. These

Snakes were not dangerous and would be kept around the properties, as they would kill the rattlesnakes, rats, and mice.

There also were lizards, toads, crickets, beetles, and of course different kinds of bugs. One bug was called a "Stink Bug"—so named because if you happened to crush them, they would generate an awful smell. There were a variety of birds, butterflies, and flying insects as well.

I had a great fascination for all these wild creatures and animals. I did avoid the harmful ones, as I knew they were dangerous. The others, I would talk to as if they could understand what I was saying, and I considered them all my wonderful friends

Which now brings me to my first of the tales in this section.

AN ANIMAL ACTIVIST AT AN EARLY AGE
Tale # 1: The Cute Little Lizard

At the age of 8, I would walk to school every day on a very long sandy road that had ruts in it made from the wheels of the neighbor's car (we did not own a car). And in the center of the road were small brush and weeds, so you would walk in one of the ruts made by the wheels of the car. This road led up to the railroad-track crossing, which I would cross over and then be in the main part of the small town. All the roads were dirt except for the main highway, which ran through the middle of the town: it was paved. I can't recall any sidewalks in the town. If there were, I don't remember them.

So off I would go on this road to school, which was located on the other side of town. I carried a brown paper bag with me, which held my lunch. All of us children brought lunches to school, and we would all eat together at noontime.

However, there was one problem with my walking to school: my parents kept getting a note from the teacher telling them that I was arriving late for class every day. Each time my parents got a note from the teacher, they would send me that much earlier to school—and still I would be late. Finally, after getting yet another note, my father decided to follow me to school (without my knowing it) to find out why I was always so late.

The next time I walked to school, after I had walked just

a small ways up the road, I happened to see a lizard getting ready to cross in front of me. So I bent over and said to the lizard, "Hello, little Lizard, you are a cute little lizard. Don't worry, I won't hurt you." And with that, I felt a sting against the back of my legs.

I turned around and there was my dad with a thin switch in his hand. I got the message immediately, and I started to run, with my dad behind me. When I slowed down, my dad gave me a little tap with the switch.* (It was not a cruel switching; actually, it was a soft, bendable twig that would cause a light sting to the bare legs that only lasted a second, and never was felt again.). My father did not have me run very long, just long enough so I would get the message, which I did. And my morning talking sessions came to an end, not only with wildlife but with humans, as well.

Later on, my mother found out the reason I was late was not only because I was talking to all the creatures I met as I went to school, but also because I was having daily visits with an elderly semi-blind couple, who sat out on their front porch every

---

* When I was growing up, switching was the traditional form of punishment with the majority of people. These days, I am aware that some of the whippings were carried to an extreme, which I feel very sad about. Reading about my being switched and spanked in a couple of additional tales may upset you, as well, and I apologize for that. However, it was not considered child abuse at that time to use a switch or spanking as a form of punishment. As soon as it was over with, we never felt it anymore. At the time, it was just punishment and that was all; and for me, it never harmed me emotionally.·

morning. The way my mother found out about this was that when she went to visit this elderly couple, they told her how much they missed my stopping and talking with them every morning on the way to school, as I always brightened up their day and they hoped I was okay. End of story.

Tale # 2: "Kay, What Kind of Mice Do We Have?"

It was a fall day. I was in the house, playing, when my father came home from town, carrying a paper sack in his hand. Always hungry, I thought it was something to eat; so I hurried over to him as he sat down on the chair next to the kitchen table, and as I watched, he pulled out these strange wooden-looking things from the bag. I was disappointed at there being no food, and yet very curious as to why my dad would buy these strange-looking pieces of wood.

I asked him what they were, and he explained to me: "These are mouse traps, and they are going to catch the mice."

"Why do you want to do that?" I asked.

He replied, "We can't have mice in the house. We have to get rid of them."

My dad went to the refrigerator, took out a large piece of cheese, and came back and sat down again at the table. Then he took one of the wooden traps and proceeded to show me how the traps would work, by placing a piece of cheese on the little metal latch attached to a thick metal spring. As soon as the mouse took the cheese, the spring would come down over the mouse's neck and kill it.

"Daddy, how can you kill them?" I asked him. He said he didn't like to do it, but the mice were getting into everything and that was the only way he could get rid of them. He also mentioned to me to keep my fingers away from the trap, as I might lose a finger.

So I watched him as he set up the traps. And then I went around with him to every room, and saw where he was placing them. After my father had finished placing the traps, he put on his railroad cap and left for work. He worked the 4:00 pm to 12:00 am shift in the railroad yards, at that time.

I watched him leave; and after he was gone, making sure that my mom was not around to see me, I got a long, thick stick from outside in the yard, and then I went around to all our rooms, put the stick on the metal latch with the cheese, and set off all the mouse traps.

My dad did not bother to look at the traps when he came home that night, as he was tired and ready for bed. But the next day, he got up to see how many mice he had caught. He couldn't believe his eyes! The traps were sprung and the cheese was gone, but no mice were in the traps. The next afternoon, he went around and reset the traps. After he left for work, I went around and again sprung all the traps with the stick.

My father did this a couple more times more. Finally, he was so bewildered by the empty traps and missing cheese that he said to my mom, "Kay, what kind of mice do we have, anyway? I can't understand this. The traps are sprung and the cheese is gone— how do they do it?" My father never caught on that *I* was the one springing the traps, and he finally gave up. I was so very happy that no mice were killed.

My Dad ended up getting a cat instead, and I was so

happy about having a new pet (not realizing the purpose behind his gift).

Tale # 3: Duck Hunting with My Father

My father had a couple of days off from work, and decided that he would like to go duck hunting and get a nice duck for our meal. So he asked me if I would like to go with him. I said yes! I was thrilled that my dad felt I was big enough to go with him. (I don't remember how old I was at this time, only that I was old enough to go with him and yet small enough that he could carry me across the swamps and muddy places.) My father put on his rubber boots that went clear up to his hips, a heavy shirt, his railroad jacket, and hat, and was all ready to leave. My mom had bundled me up, as well, as it was fall and there was a nip of frost in the air. Mom also fixed us a lunch and waved goodbye as we left to go duck hunting.

Living in a small town, we were right in the area where the lagoon and swamps were, and we could get there by walking. We finally got to the spot that looked just right to make a blind for geese. My father and I were scrunched down in the tall brush, and he took the gun in his hand, waiting for the geese to fly by. I don't remember how long we stayed there waiting for them, but finally, not seeing any geese, my father got up and picked me up to carry me over the swamp to another area to look for ducks.

We were gone all day, my father often carrying me so that my feet would not get wet. And finally, as the sun was getting ready to set, my father decided that it was hopeless to stay around any longer. I told him that I was too tired to walk any more, so he picked me up and carried me all the way back home on his back (which we used to call a "piggy-back ride").

When we entered the house, my mom asked my dad, "Ray, did you get any ducks?" My dad said, "Kay it was the strangest thing: not only did I not get a goose or a duck, but I didn't even *see* one. This has never happened to me, before."

I spoke up and said, "Mama, I'm sure glad he didn't. I was praying all the time we were gone that we wouldn't see any."

That was the last time my father ever went hunting.

"SCHOOL DAYS, SCHOOL DAYS, GOOD OLD GOLDEN-RULE DAYS"

Why I never liked going to school when I was young is a question that's hard for me to answer. I really can't say why. I don't know if it was from boredom, or that I would rather be out playing and having fun.

I was smart enough. However, my report cards showed low grading when it came to conduct in school. I did receive high marks for politeness, social behavior, hygiene; but the "poor conduct" grade was due to not paying attention to the teacher, and acting up in class to make others laugh. I did love to read and to hear stories that the teacher would tell and draw pictures. And of course, I loved recreation time.

Tale #1: It Pays to Tell the Truth

During my early school years, there were times when I felt bored in class and longed to be outside playing—or at least trying to find something interesting or exciting to do outside of the classroom. So naturally, I longed for an opportunity to get out of school.

One day, when I was in third grade, I noticed that any child who went up to the teacher and said they had a sore throat was sent home. Wow! This was my chance to get out of school. My lucky day had come.

I went up to the teacher and said, "I have a sore throat." The teacher replied, "Are you sure you have a sore throat?" Rubbing the outside of my neck with my hand and putting a painful look on my face, I replied, "Oh yes, it is very sore." She looked at me and said, "Well then, you had better go home."

I went out of the classroom still rubbing my neck with the same painful look on my face. After all, I still had to make this look convincing. However, as soon as I was out of sight from the school, I skipped all the way home, happy as a lark. Free from school—what a wonderful feeling!

But this feeling did not last very long. My mother saw me coming up the road and met me at the door; and with a quizzical look on her face, she asked me what was wrong and why was I coming home. Putting on the sickest expression I could muster, I replied: "Oh, I'm so sick, I have a sore throat and it hurts." My mom looked at me and said, "You don't *look* very sick to me." Then she put her hand on my head and said, "You don't have a fever, and your face is not even flushed. Let me check your throat." Oh-oh, now I was in trouble! I knew she was about to discover the truth that I really didn't have a sore throat. And I had no way of getting out of it.

My mother came back with a spoon in one hand and a flashlight in the other. She would always check for a sore throat by using the handle of the spoon to depress the back of my tongue and then turn on the flashlight so she could have a good view of my throat. As she looked down my throat, she heaved a big sigh of disgust. Her doubt had been confirmed: no sore throat –no sick child. She quickly turned me around and headed me out the door, saying, "Go back to school and don't you dare come home until it time for you to do so."

Unhappily, I headed back to school. All was in vain. As soon as I entered the classroom, the teacher ran over to me and said, "You are not supposed to be here. Now go right back home." A smile came onto my face as I left the school and headed happily back home.

When my mother saw me coming back, she became very upset and came out. Taking my hand, she said, "Young lady"— she always said that to me when she was ready to scold me or threaten me—"I'm taking you back to school to make certain that you stay there!" Trotting beside her to keep up with her fast steps (she could really walk fast when she was angry), I started to cry, and said, "But mama, the teacher sent me home!" Mother kept on going, giving my hand a tug of disbelief.

We reached the schoolroom, and again the teacher came running over, saying to my mother, "Your girl cannot come in here." Taken back by the teacher's action and comment, my mother replied, "Why not? Eloise doesn't have a sore throat at all." The teacher replied, "We are not allowed to let any child who complains of a sore throat in school until they have seen the doctor, and have a written consent that the child is well. I am sorry, Mrs. Aitken, but you will have to take your daughter back home."

The reason I could not go back to school was that two separate cases of diphtheria had broken out in the town, and any child complaining of a sore throat was sent home, as all precautions were being taken to prevent an epidemic. The teacher had to follow the mandate that was given to her. If a child complained of a sore throat and was sent home, the child had to be quarantined until the doctor gave a certificate of release. But we did not *have* a doctor in our town. We did not have a car, either; and my father was out of town working as an Engineer on the Railroad trains. This meant that my mother would have to wait until the doctor came to town so he could examine me. I can't remember how long it was before he came to the school to examine the children who went home with a sore throat.

My mother, being very upset at the news that the teacher

gave her, took me by the hand and brought me home. When we got inside the door, she said to me, "All right, young lady—you said you were sick, and sick you shall be. Now go to your room and crawl into bed, and you will stay there until I tell you that you can get up and leave your room."

Oh boy, I hadn't bargained for this. Even to this day, I remember so well how I regretted my actions. I crawled into bed and looked at the four walls, and started to cry. I don't actually remember how many days I stayed in bed—maybe one, maybe more. All I remember is that I would have much rather been in school than in bed.

Not having any brothers or sisters to distract me from my "torture" of being in bed, all I could do was lie there and read the little pictorial storybook about Noah's Ark. By the time I left my bed, I had memorized all the words in the book. Even to this day, I remember some of it:

> "Once upon a time, they say,
> The rain came down day after day,
> Pouring, pouring from the sky
> Until not a spot on earth was dry.
> So Noah built an ark so wide
> That all the animals could stay inside.
> Listen to their noisy den.
> Look, each one of them has a twin.
> Up the gangplank unto the Ark
> The noisy cows moo and the little dogs bark.
> Here comes the turkey in full array—
> So glad it isn't Thanksgiving day."
> Etc. . . .

Yes, a very miserable, unhappy child learned a good lesson: it doesn't pay to tell a lie to get out of school.

But was the lesson learned?

Tale # 2: Sick Again!

Well, I should say that the lesson was *not* learned. Yes, you guessed it: another episode about my telling a lie to get out of school.

I was around 11 or 12 years of age at that time. As you already know, I didn't care much for going to school, although I did love my teachers and my friends. But I didn't like the discipline of having to sit still and do school work for a whole day. I found it boring when outside, there were so much more interesting things to do and see than study.

I was still living in the same town and attending the same school. It was a lovely day outside, and as I looked out the window I knew that was where I wanted to be— not in here with my nose in a book. So, not learning from past experience (and having a different teacher, this time), I decided to be sick again.

I had it all figured out. Instead of going home, this time I would just fool around outside until I knew that school would be out. So I went to my teacher and asked if I could go home because I wasn't feeling a bit well: my stomach was hurting me. The teacher, feeling most sorry for me, said, "Of course, dear, you may leave." I had a bicycle by this time, which I would ride to school, so I jumped on it and I was off on my merry way.

Well, time happened to get away from me, and I didn't realize that school had been out for some time. When I got home and walked in the door, there was my mother not looking very pleased with me! She said to me, "Where have you been?" I said I had to stay after school – I thought I could get away with this explanation, as there *were* times I had to stay after school and write on the blackboard, "I will not talk during class" over and over again.

However, my mom did not buy this. "Young lady," she said to me in a very stern voice, "I just now got home from the grocery store—and whom do you think I met while I was in the store?" I shrugged my shoulders as if to say, "I don't know."

My mom went on, saying, "It was your teacher. She asked me how you were feeling, and that she hoped you were feeling much better. I said to your teacher, 'My daughter is fine, why do you ask?' She then told me that you had left just before lunchtime because you weren't feeling well and had a stomach ache. So I told your teacher, 'When Eloise comes home, she is going to *wish* she had come home with a stomach ache.'"

Yes, I did pay the price for lying and playing hooky, as I couldn't do what I loved the most. As punishment, I was not allowed to go to the movie theater that Saturday night. Well, that ended my telling lies and playing hooky from school. To use an old cliché, I learned that "Crime doesn't pay"!

PART VI

TALES OF ADVENTURES
OR MISADVENTURES

THE RACE IN THIRD GRADE

There is nothing like a proud mother when her only child wins second place in a race.

I took part in the annual grade-school picnic at the close of the school year. I was eight years of age at that time, and this was my very first race. The bonnet I was wearing that my mom had made for me kept bobbing up and down over my eyes as I ran. But that did not stop me; I just kept running until I reached the finish line. They gave me a red ribbon for coming in second place. I was so happy and excited with my second-place win.

I could hardly wait to get home to show my mother, and when the picnic was over I went running home as fast I could go. I ran into the house and proudly presented my mom with my red ribbon. My mother was so proud of me and happy for me that she promptly snipped a small piece off the red ribbon and placed it opposite my baby picture in the locket that she wore around her neck.

My mother could hardly wait to share the news with her friends that her darling girl had won second place in the race; and so she did. One day, she was visiting with one of her friends and telling her the exciting news, while opening her locket to show off the piece of red ribbon. Her friend happened to pose the question, "How many were in the race?" My mother had never thought to ask me, so she turned to me and asked,

"How many were in the race?"

I very proudly replied: "TWO."

HELP, I'M DYING!

In a small town in the early 1940s, we kids had a lot of freedom and a lot of open space to run around in to play or go exploring. There was a large dirt canal that was always full of water, which the farmers would use for irrigating their farmland. We kids loved to go swimming in the canal. Our favorite spot was where the canal was dammed with wooden slats on a concrete base so that the amount of water could be regulated. For us, it was it was like a mini falls. In fact, that was how I learned how to swim. I would go down the falls, which seemed to carry me a good distance, and kick and flail my arms. And it wasn't long before I got the hang of swimming.

On the side of the canals, there were some places where the water would run over the banks onto an area that would be real gooey with thick, slimy mud. This one day, I thought it would be fun to go wading in it, which I did. The feeling of the mud slipping through my toes, all the way up my legs to my thighs as I was walking, felt oh so gooey and slimy. And oh, it was so much fun – I just loved it.

After a while, though, it was no fun any more, so I decided to crawl out of the mud onto the bank of the canal. I could that see my legs were full of mud, so I got back into the water to wash the mud off. To my surprise and dismay, the mud would not come off my legs. I couldn't figure out why I couldn't wipe it off with hands, so I got out of the water and found a small flat piece of wood and started to scrape the mud off my legs.

All of a sudden, I could see blood rolling down my leg. I scraped the mud off my leg. Again, more blood came rolling down. It was then I realized that something was sucking the blood out my legs. I scraped again, and more blood started. I was terrified, as the more I scraped, the more the blood came out of me. I just knew I was bleeding to death.

Leaving the kids behind, I started running for home, screaming all the way, "Help me, help me, I'm dying, I'm dying!" My father heard my cries from inside the house and came out to meet me. As soon as he saw my legs, he knew right at that moment that my legs were covered with leeches, also called bloodsuckers. So he calmly told me that I was not dying, and that I would be okay. "Are you sure Daddy?" I asked. He reassured me again. He had me sit on a chair and proceeded to remove the leeches with a bottle of turpentine. As he applied it, the leeches dropped off my legs.

From that day on I never ventured into that muddy area again. I had learned the lesson well.

THE END OF THE WORLD

My Godfather, Harry Grace, was a "good practicing Catholic." Knowing that there was not a Catholic Church for miles around, and being very concerned about his Godchild not having a Catholic Church to worship in, and so not able to go to religion classes—he felt it was his duty to see that I was brought up as a "good Catholic." So he mailed my mother the "Baltimore Catechism" for me to memorize and learn all the answers in the book. I was in the fourth grade at the time.

The first part of the Catechism had questions such as:

Question: "Who made you?" Answer: "God made me!"

Question: "Why did God make you?" Answer: "To Know Him, Love Him, and serve Him in this world—so that we may be Happy in this life and in the next."

Also in this book was a section on sin and the kinds of sin. There was also a picture, along with this explanation, of three milk bottles. One milk bottle was all white (this is what your soul looked like without any sin). The next bottle had black dots in it (this was your soul in lesser sin). And then there was the bottle that was all black (this was a soul in very, very bad sin, called "Mortal sin"). If you died with this sin, you could not go to heaven. Instead, you would go into the fiery furnace called hell.

My mother, trying to follow the admonitions of my Godfather, this one spring day told me about the Catholic practice of Lent, which lasted for 40 days. So my mother suggested that in order to show Jesus how much I loved him, I should give up something that I loved during Lent. Since I loved candy so much, I decided to give up candy. So unhappily I said yes, I would do it, as I wanted to show Jesus that I really loved him.

One Friday during this period of Lent, all of us school kids were talking about the article in the newspaper that someone in the sixth grade had brought to school. The article was about a woman's prediction that the world would come to an end the next day, on the following Saturday. We really were wondering what it would be like, and how and what would happen if it was really true and the world came to an end. All of us kids were filled with both fear and excitement about this prediction.

At home that evening, I was assured by mom that the world was not going to end, and that the woman who had made the prediction was not all there in her thinking. I wanted to believe my mother; yet at the same time, there was this question looming in my mind: could she really know? Was the woman in the newspaper a fortuneteller who could predict the future? And was she right?

That next day, Saturday, three of my friends came to take me with them to one of our favorite places to play: by the beacon light for planes that might have to land in case of an emergency. There was an asphalt-covered runway for the landing strip; and since there were no other buildings around, it made a nice place for us to play hopscotch and Jacks, draw pictures with our colored chalk, or play other games.

On this day, my friends had brought with them a bag of candy: orange gumdrop slices made to look like real orange slices. My friends wanted to share some of their candy with me. However, since it was Lent and I had promised to give up candy for Jesus, I kept refusing, even though I wanted some so badly. Oh, that candy looked so yummy! My mouth was watering from the thought of how good it would taste. And so the next time my friends offered me the orange slice, I just couldn't refuse. I took it and ate it. It tasted so delicious!

But after I had eaten it, I felt so guilty. I knew I had sinned. I saw my soul looking just like that black milk bottle in the Catechism – oh no, now my soul was in mortal sin! Since my friends were not Catholic, I did not want to say anything to them about this; nor did I dare say a word to my mom about my soul being black from breaking my promise to Jesus and that my soul was in mortal sin.

That night as I was sleeping, I was awakened by sounds of thunder. And as I opened my eyes, the room was all lit up with light. I looked out the bedroom window, and all the sky was white with light. I had never seen anything like this before. The thunder was so loud, and the light was just staying in the sky, so I knew it was the end of the world, just like the woman had predicted (I had never seen what they call "sheet lightning" before)—and here I was, my soul as black as that milk bottle—Oh no! I was in mortal sin and was going to go to hell.

I hurried and jumped out of bed and got down on my knees, buried my head in the coverings, and prayed aloud, saying, "Oh God, please forgive me - please don't let me go to hell. Oh please forgive me, I don't want to go to hell." Then I crawled back into bed, pulling the covers over my head, trembling in fear.

Not long after, the storm ceased. I found out it was not the end of the world, after all. I was one happy girl—and even happier when I found out eating that eating that candy was *not* a sin. To this very day, every time I see the same candy orange slices in the stores I remember this tale so well.

OH, WHAT A GREAT CHRISTMAS GIFT

Every Christmas, I looked forward to opening up my Christmas gift that my grandmother sent me. I knew she would always have a doll for me in my package, and I just loved the dolls. When Grandma's Christmas package would arrive at the Post Office and my mom would bring it home, I was always so excited to see it. I could hardly wait for Christmas day to come so I could see the doll that my Grandma had for me.

Finally, Christmas day arrived. As I opened up her package, I saw a beautiful doll.

However, what I saw alongside it was the best gift of all: one piece of Double Bubble Gum. If this tale were a movie, as I looked at the Double Bubble Gum there would be fireworks going off and great lights all around for this amazing gift. There it was, in all its splendor! Yes, Double Bubble Gum.

Now you may ask, why was this bubble gum the best gift ever? Well, I will explain.

Living in a small town that had only one grocery store, we kids did not have much choice in bubble gum. For some reason, the store clerk stopped getting the Double Bubble Gum that we kids just loved. Instead, he started purchasing this horrible-tasting bubble gum, which we would chew but really did not like at all. It tasted really bad; in fact, it tasted horrible. Yet we chewed it so that we could enjoy blowing bubbles.

I hurried and put the bubble gum in my mouth right away, and chewed and chewed and savored the delicious taste. Oh, what great flavor that Double Bubble Gum had! And the bubbles were so easy to blow; it was not tough like the other gum. All that day, except for when I ate, I kept the gum in my mouth and chewed it. It was heaven on earth. That night, when I went to bed, I carefully stuck it on the top of my metal bed frame that was behind my pillows.

The next morning, the first thing I did when I woke up was to take the gum off the bed frame, put it in my mouth, and started chewing it again. Oh, how great it was! I could hardly wait to go to my girlfriend's house to tell her about my wonderful gift.

That afternoon, I got on my bicycle with the gum still in my mouth and headed for my girlfriend's house. When I got inside, I quickly showed her my Double Bubble Gum that my Grandma had sent me. When she saw it, she said, "Oh, you are so lucky to have Double Bubble Gum. I sure wish *I* had gotten some." So I said to her, "Would you like to chew it while I am here?" And I took it out of my mouth and gave it to her. Smiling with joy, she gleefully took the gum and put it in her own mouth. All that afternoon, I let her chew my gum. When it came time for me to go home, she sadly took the gum out of her mouth and gave it back to me. I put it in my mouth and happily rode back home.

For I don't remember for how long, every night I would

take the gum out of my mouth and place it on the metal frame of my bed. By this time, the flavor was gone. But that didn't matter; it still blew wonderful bubbles. This one morning when I woke up to go to school, to my horror I could not find my gum anywhere. I looked all over and still could not find it. It was not in the bed covers, behind the bed, or on the floor beneath the bed. I couldn't figure what had happened to my gum.

Well, I was still young enough that my mother would comb my hair every day. When she started combing my hair, the mystery of the lost gum was solved: it had fallen off the frame of the bed during the night, and landed in my hair, where it was stuck right in the back of my head at the top. The only recourse my mom had was to take the scissors and cut off my hair in that spot where the gum had entangled itself in my hair.

I started crying—not because I would be going to school with a tonsure (bald spot) on the top of my head, but because that was the end of my Double Bubble Gum.

SUMMER TIME IN THE SMALL TOWN

I loved summers. Not only was I out of school, but also summers meant the freedom we had as kids to explore, swim in the canal, take bike rides, climb trees, and play ball. Once in awhile we would build a bonfire out in the middle of the dirt road (it was safe, as there was no traffic and we had adult supervision). One of the boys who played with us all the time was the instigator for us to sneak into his father's field of corn, where we stole ears of corn to put in our bonfire, husk and all. After we played our games around the bonfire, we would happily eat the burnt corn.

Not having any brothers or sisters, I made up for it by making my dog, two cats, one rabbit, two turtles, a toad in the water box outside and a stuffed panda, that went to bed with me every night into my siblings. I would be so happy when a cousin around my age would come to visit during the summer, as it helped to make up for the loneliness of not having a brother or sister.

The truth of the matter is that not only did I love having my cousins come but I also loved having relatives come to visit from other states, as well. Since we didn't have any relatives at all living in our state, it meant that their visits would be on a yearly basis, as where we lived, you came either by train or by car. I was always so thrilled when I heard that some of our family members were coming to visit us. In fact I would run around the whole town telling everyone, "My Relatives are coming! My Relatives are coming!"

A VISIT FROM COUSIN LARRY

One summer, my Aunt, whom I called my "other Mother," sent her son who was close to my age to come and spend the summer with us. She felt it would be good for him to have a change from city life in Los Angeles, and also to experience country life, with its wide-open spaces. Hearing the news of cousin Larry coming to live with us for the summer, I got on my bicycle and rode around town; and to anyone I saw who was outside as I passed by, I would yell, "My Cousin Larry is coming!"

We both were young in age, and it didn't take long for us to discover that we were going to get along just fine. I just knew we would have a great summer together, playing and doing all my fun activities. My Cousin Larry took to small-town life very quickly and didn't seem to be a bit homesick.

THE HAYSTACK

Shortly before Cousin Larry came, we had just moved to another house in the town, which I really loved, even though it did not have running hot water in it or an indoor bathroom. However, it did have a large yard with a wooden walkway. There was an apple tree, and also a large barn that held the landlord's milk cows inside at night.

There was also a very large fenced-in area around the barn that kept the cows from straying away when they were outside. Next to the barn was a huge haystack, the cows' main source of food. I so loved looking at the cows and talking to them. There was enough land for my father to plant a large garden, and it even was large enough for me to have my watermelon patch, as well.

My Cousin Larry had been here for a couple of days, and we already were having a great time together. My father happened to have time off from work for a couple of days, and so used this time not only to entertain us but also to work out in his garden.

This one day, my father was going to work in his garden. Noticing that Larry and I were out playing in the backyard as well, he decided to bring out two large bottles of soda to us (we called it "soda pop"). Larry and I were out by the barn and haystack, playing cowboys (we kids loved Western movies and cowboys). When my father brought us the large bottles of soda pop to drink while we were playing, needless to say we were absolutely delighted. Soda was a luxury for us kids; our main drink was punch.

Now that we had the soda pop, we decided to make the haystack our Saloon (bar), where we would drink our soda pop. Our broomsticks were our horses; and, being cowboys, we would come back on our broomsticks and go straight to the Saloon, where we would quench our thirst with a sip of soda from the bottle.

While my father was working in the garden, he would look every once in a while over to where we were playing; and he noticed that we would take the soda pop out of the haystack, then take the cap off the bottles, take a sip of the sodas, put the cap back on, and then place our pop bottles back inside the haystack. We kept doing this for some time.

Finally, my dad's curiosity got the better of him, so he came over to us and asked, "Don't you kids *like* the soda pop I brought you?" To which I answered, "Oh yes, Daddy, we love the soda pop very much. We are only doing what Mr. Dunston does every day when he comes here."

Mr. Dunston was the landlord of our house, and every morning and night he would come to feed his cows. He would go over to the haystack; and before he picked up his pitchfork to gather the hay, he would reach inside the haystack and take out a bottle of whiskey. Then he would remove the cap, take a huge gulp of the booze, and then proceed to put the bottle back inside the haystack. He would also do the same thing when he was leaving to go home: he would take another large gulp of whiskey and walk away with a big smile on his face.

I know you have already surmised that Mr. Dunston did not want anyone to know of his drinking. However, there is even more to that story than meets the eye. It was against Mr. Dunston's religion to drink alcohol. In fact, drinking anything of an alcoholic nature was strictly forbidden; and if anyone should be caught drowning their thirst with an alcoholic beverage, they would be severely chastised by the head of the church. The haystack provided a perfect, safe place for him to quench his thirst, so to speak, without anyone finding out.

When Mr. Dunston would come to feed his cows and imbibe the whiskey, he never knew that he had a "Peeping Tom" watching him. And even though I was young, I sensed that he was doing something he shouldn't be doing, so I never told anyone. It was my own private secret until that day when my father saw us imitating him.

PART VII

LOVE OF THEATER AND ACTING
AT AN EARLY AGE

From the time I can remember, I was singing and dancing, pretending I was on stage. I would also include my childhood friends to join me in being part of my acting and musical life. Our stage was anything from a living room to being on top of a hay wagon that was just sitting there with no hay in it (it made such a wonderful stage for singing and dancing).

I also found that the garages made an excellent place for my theater. On two different occasions, while presenting my plays in the garages, right in the middle of the play my mother would come into the garage and take me outside, where I received a good spanking.

Now, why would my mother ever do something like that? Did I suffer from Child Abuse? You will soon find out in my next two tales.

THE PLAY IN OUR OLD UNUSED GARAGE

I picked just the perfect spot in the garage for the stage. Then, with the help of a younger boy called Sonny and my two girlfriends, we went out collecting wooden crates for the kids to sit on.

After we had set up our theater, I had my two girlfriends and Sonny be actors in my play. I had them go over their parts, which had more movement than words. However, they would have lines to say at the right time, and they would learn them by rote while we were rehearsing the play. (Of course, there was a lot of prompting going on during the production of a play.) After I felt that the three actors had rehearsed their parts enough, and it being lunchtime, we all left for lunch. The two girls and Sonny headed on home and promised me that they would come right back after they ate. Which they did, except for Sonny.

I got the two girls to come with me to gather up the kids to come see my play. The way I would entice the kids to come was by telling them that they would get a free drink of Kool-Aid. In those days, Kool-Aid was the kids' favorite drink. It was a fruit-flavored powder in a packet, which you would open and then pour the flavored powder into a large pitcher. Then you would add a cup of sugar and fill the pitcher with cold water. You would stir it until the fruit powder and sugar were all dissolved – and your Kool-Aid was now ready to drink.

I would fill two large pitchers and put them in the

refrigerator until it was time for the play to start. Mind you, we didn't have that many kids come—but it still was enough kids for me, and that was all that mattered. We three girls were happy at our success in getting some kids to come to our play; and before it began, I went around passing out the small paper cups of Kool-Aid for them to drink while watching our play.

The kids were all seated on the crates, drinking their Kool-Aid and waiting for the play to begin. I was worried because Sonny had not shown up yet. A couple of moments later, I was relieved—Sonny arrived just in time for me to get him ready to go onstage so the play could go on. After all, he was the main actor—the star of our play.

The plot was that a young boy was to have fallen over a cliff and rolled down the mountainside. Then the two girls would see him lying on the ground in great pain, and they would run over to the injured boy to help him and keep him from dying. The play would end with him completely healed and thanking the girls for saving him from death. I was so proud of myself for the way I had gotten Sonny ready for his big part; and from his appearance, he really did look like he had just rolled down the mountainside.

We had no curtain to open or close, so I went out on the stage and announced that the play was ready to begin. Sonny rolled out onto the stage just as we had rehearsed, and the girls came running from the other side of the stage to help the injured boy who had rolled down the mountainside. The play was going along so well, when all of a sudden the boy's mother came in, yanked him up from the floor—and out of the garage they went. Needless to say, the play ended, due to the loss of the main character.

The next thing I knew, here came my mom, very upset. She took me by the arm, and with the other hand she gave me swats on my bottom. I did not as of yet know why I was getting spanked, until I heard her say to me, "Shame on you for getting Sonny and his clothes so filthy dirty."

Now, what was so bad about the young boy being so dirty that I would be getting a spanking because of it? Well, for two reasons: The first was that when Sonny went home for lunch, his mother gave him a bath and dressed him up in his best clothes to take him to the doctor for his annual checkup later on that afternoon.

The second reason: when he came back for our play, I hurried and took him around to the back of the garage, where there was an old stovepipe that had been thrown away. It was filled with greasy black soot that had collected in it from the burning stove. I put my hand inside the discarded stovepipe, took out this greasy black soot, and smeared it all over Sonny's face and clothes—after all, he had to look authentic, like he had tumbled down the mountainside.

Sonny's mother had let him come back to my house, and she had planned on coming over to pick him up when it was time to take him to the doctor. What she *didn't* plan on was my play, and my smearing greasy soot all over him and ruining his clothes.

My mother knew I was putting on a play in the garage, since this was not the first time I had done this, and she never bothered checking out what we were doing. You can imagine how my mother felt when Sonny's mother brought him to the front door of our home, all covered in greasy soot, and Sonny's mother yelled at my mom, "Look what your girl did to my boy—just look at his good clothes!—They are ruined!"

ANOTHER PLAY—ANOTHER SPANKING

It was summer time, and like every summer, my mom and I were staying with my grandmother. On the block where my grandmother lived was an alley way, consisting of a small dirt road that ran right through the middle of the block separating the backyards of the houses on both sides of the alley.

The neighbor's yard alongside of Grandma's backyard was beautiful, with the most gorgeous roses ever to be seen. Right across the alley from this lovely garden was my uncle's garage, with its doors opening up onto the alley. Now, this garage was going to be just perfect for my play—it was empty, since my uncle was out of town—and my play would be over before he got back.

This time in my play, I had my Cousin Nellie (who was my age) and her younger brother be the actors, along with a couple of Nellie's girlfriends. As with all my plays, I also had Nellie and her brother go out and round up the kids for my audience.

Now mind you, this was going to be a very dramatic play! My actress was dying, and as she was doing so, I was going to drop rose petals down on her as if they were falling from heaven. I found that three orange crates put together end-to -end, and one of the two white sheets that I secretly took out of my grandmother's closet to cover them, made a perfect place for her to die on. Then I strung up a rope behind the crates, and put the other white sheet over the rope so that I could stand on a crate behind the sheet and gently drop the rose petals down on top of her without my audience seeing me.

My cousins did a good job of rounding up the kids to be the audience for my play; and of course, the offering of a drink of Kool-Aid helped out, as well.

The dramatic moment of my play was now beginning. My actress was lying on her cot, dying, and I was behind the white sheet, standing on a crate, gently dropping down real rose petals on her while the other two actors were crying beside the dying woman. So there I was, standing on the crate, taking out the rose petals that I had gathered—and as I was dropping them down over the white sheet, I was so happy that all was going so well.

All of a sudden, as I was dropping these petals, I was pulled off the crate by a hand that grabbed me around the waist. And before I knew it, my mother had me and began slapping my bottom as hard as she could, without my having a clue as to why she started doing this, until I heard her saying, "How could you do this? How could you do it? You destroyed all of Mr. Fanto's roses."

Now, you may be thinking that this was pretty harsh punishment for such a deed. After all, I was only a child and his rose bushes would bloom again. Yes, true, they *would* bloom again. The huge problem was that for months, Mr. Fanto had been nurturing his rose bushes so that he could produce prize-winning roses—which he did have, at that time, and was going to present his prize-winning roses at the Rose Show the following day in hopes of winning the Blue Ribbon.

I'm sure you can just picture Mr. Fanto in your mind when he came out into his yard to find all his roses gone, and how devastating it was for him. From his yard across the alley, he could see me through the open doors of the garage, dropping the rose petals. Yours truly had gone into his yard and pulled all the petals off every single rose, leaving only the bud on the stem. There were five different rose bushes, each one a different color—red, pink, white, and yellow. I did not realize, when I did this horrible misdeed, that they were Prize Roses, nor did I think he would mind, as I had left the stems for more roses, and those petals were so important for the dying scene in my dramatic play.

ON STAGE:
THE KINDERGARTEN GRADUATION

This tale happened when I was in High School helping Sister Mary Margaret with her Kindergarten Graduation. And since we are talking about plays on stage, this tale definitely has something to do with being on stage—and with me as well, as you will soon find out.

When I was in tenth grade, the Catholic Sister who was our teacher in Religion Class asked me if I would help Sister Mary Margaret with her Kindergarten Graduation Class on the following weekend. I told Sister that I would be happy to help out. I felt so good that she had picked me from among the rest of the girls in my class, as I loved anything to do with the Stage.

Sister Mary Margaret was a small Irish nun with a very thick brogue. Listening to her, you didn't need to ask her what country she was from—clearly, it was Ireland. Sister taught her children their lines by rote. She would go over and over each line with them, again and again.

We high-school kids would get such a kick out of the Kindergarten children saying their lines onstage. Not only were they really cute, standing there, but also when they were reciting their lines they were doing so with an Irish brogue. What was so funny about it all was that the parents of the children on stage were not from Ireland but from Mexico.

THE DAY OF GRADUATION

The weekend came for the Kindergarten Graduation. I was there helping Sister Mary Margaret get the kids dressed in their costumes for the parts they would be doing onstage. Sister had just put four of the kids onstage. Then she came back to where I was and asked, "Where is Johnny?"

Just then, lo and behold, in through the outside door came Johnny's mom holding him by the hand; and in his other hand, he was holding an 8-1/2-by-11 white card with the letter "O" on it.

Sister said to me, "Quick, go get him and put him on stage while I finish dressing these kids for the next act." I took the little boy, who was still holding his large card with the large letter "O" on it, opened the curtain on the side, and gently pushed him onto the stage. Then I went back to where Sister and the other kids were; and as I got there, all of a sudden, the whole audience started breaking out into peals of laughter.

Sister said to me, "Go out in front and see why they are laughing. They shouldn't be laughing at all! This is a serious piece." So I went out in front—and there were the five kids standing in a straight row, each one holding a card with a letter on it in their hands, looking down at the audience. As soon as I saw what the cards were supposed to spell, I realized that I had put Johnny at the top of the line whereas he should have been at the bottom of the line.

For this is what I saw when I looked at the cards—

"O H E L L"

instead of—

"H E L L O."

PART VIII

WORKING DURING
MY HIGH-SCHOOL YEARS

A BABYSITTING JOB

Until I was a senior in high school, one of my main means of making money was babysitting. I babysat for this one family for a couple of weekends in the summer time, taking care of their one-year-old, a three-year-old, and a five-year old—all boys—while their parents were away on a weekend from Friday to Sunday night. I laugh to myself now when I think of this one incident that happened when I was babysitting these three boys.

It was late afternoon, and the two older boys were outside playing in the backyard. I was keeping a good watch on them to be sure they were safe, as they were playing, when the little one-year-old boy woke up from his nap and started crying.

I went into the bedroom to take him out of his crib, and was changing his diapers when the five-year-old came running into the bedroom and said, "I brought you some marbles that I found outside. I put them on the table."

I said, "Okay," and continued changing the one-year-old. When I had finished, I picked him up and brought him into the kitchen to put him in his highchair for a wee snack. After I made sure that the little one was safely strapped in his high-chair, I turned to go get him his snack—when to my horror, I saw all these bug-like creatures crawling all over on top of the kitchen table. I screamed when I first saw them, scaring the kids, as I did not know what they were and was afraid they might be poisonous and might bite as well. I had never saw anything like them before.

I got the brush and dustpan, and as I went to brush them into the pan, they all curled up into a tight ball and started rolling all over the table. Still frightened by them, I squealed each time one would fall on the floor by my foot as I was trying to brush them into the dustpan. (The little boys must have thought I was crazy.) I then gathered these critters up from the table and floor into the dustpan, and holding it with my right hand extended as far away from my body as I could, I took them outside and threw them in the bushes. (Actually, I threw the dustpan into the bushes along with them.) Finally, with much relief, I went back into the kitchen. There, I found the two older boys still standing there, their eyes as big as they could be. As I looked at them, I knew they were awe-struck at this babysitter's nutty behavior.

I found out later that these creatures are called "Rolly Pollies," or "Pill Bugs," because they roll up into a tiny ball when they get startled. They do this to protect themselves. The article I recently found when researching them said that "the back is like a hard plate—like a suit of armor that protects them from being harmed."

WORKING AT ZESTO'S DRIVE-IN

Working at Zesto's was only a summer job for senior high-school kids. It was called a Drive-In, but it was not built for cars to drive up to the window. Instead, the customers would have to get out of their parked cars and stand outside at an open window in the building and place their orders, then wait for the order to be filled. Most times, the customers would sit in their car for their order and then come back to see if their order was ready for them to pick up.

Zesto's was a popular place for high school and college kids. It was much faster than a restaurant, and required no tips. The kids also loved the foot-long hot dog and Sloppy Joe hamburgers. These two items were the real rage, along with the famous Zesto's soft ice cream.

I was working there with one other high school girl. Both of us had just finished our training with the owner. We were shown how to swirl the soft ice cream from the machine on to the cone so that it would come to a peak at the top of the ice cream. We also had to learn the number of swirls of ice cream to put on the cone, as the cost was measured by the number of swirls. Then we learned how to make malts and milk shakes, and how to serve Sloppy Joe hamburgers. This was loose hamburger that was cooked in a seasoned tomato sauce and then placed on a large round bun. The owner worked with us for a couple of days; and when she felt that we were ready to be on our own, she gave us her number to call in case of an emergency, and then left.

I had been working there for about a month, when up to my window came Jim, one of the most popular boys in our high school. Not only was he popular, but he was extremely handsome as well. When I looked at him, I would feel my heart take an extra beat. Well, this day Jim came up to the window, smiling at me as a sign of recognition, and put in his order for two chocolate milk shakes.

I wanted to make the best impression by doing everything just perfectly, as I wanted him to feel really good about me. I felt I would have to make the best milk shakes ever—and then just maybe he might notice me even more, later on. So I went to work making the milk shakes, and when they were finished I proudly brought them to the window and—giving him a large smile—I gave him the two milkshakes. I watched him as he left; and I saw him hand a milk shake to his girlfriend though the open window of the car door.

I thought to myself, "Oh, how I wish *I* was that girlfriend! I would so love to be sitting next to him in that car and looking into his beautiful blue eyes." But my daydreaming was interrupted by another customer. As I was waiting on the customer, I saw Jim coming back with one of the milk shakes in his hand. I could tell there was something wrong by the expression on his face. My heart sank to the pit of my stomach—so much for trying to make a good impression on him!—and here he was, handing me the paper cup with the milk shake running down the side of it. At that moment I realized what I had done: as I had put the paper cup into the metal shaker, I had accidentally touched the cup against the sharp blade of the beater, which put a slit on the side of the cup near the bottom. Since the milk shake had just been mixed, I didn't notice the damage.

Jim handed me the leaking cup, and—horror of horrors!—he said to me, "I want you to know that this cup was my girlfriend's, and she now has the milk shake all over her blouse and skirt."

At this point, I am going to leave this tale.

ANOTHER ZESTO'S DRIVE-IN STORY

This tale is just like the old-time "I Love Lucy Show," as I could see this happening to her, as well.

It was the 4th of July, and I was working that day. I and the other girl that worked with me were told that we could expect a lot of people, so be prepared and have everything ready for the onslaught.

The 4th of July parade was just two blocks away from us, and after the parade we had a line of people coming to the windows. I had just taken an order for a vanilla soft ice- cream cone. I went over and picked up the cone to put it under the spout, then placed my hand on the handle to open the spout to fill the cup with the swirls of ice cream; and as I turned the handle of the spigot, to my horror the next thing I knew was that the handle of the spigot was in my hand and the soft ice cream was streaming out from the open faucet down onto the floor. Panicking, I tried to put the handle back on, but to no avail.

By this time, I was standing in soft ice cream piling around my feet. All this time, the customers were watching me and the ice cream was flowing like a fountain out of the machine. The other girl who was working girl stood beside me like a frozen statue, just looking at the ice cream pouring out of the machine onto the floor. Neither one of us knew how to turn off the machine, which just made the situation even worse.

Then I remembered the empty, large, galvanized milk can in the back room. I hurried to get the can, slipping on the soft ice cream beneath my feet on the floor, and literally skated into the back room, which was close to my machine. When I came back, I put the large can under the spigot to catch the little bit of ice cream that was still left in the machine. Need I tell you, there was no vanilla ice cream to offer the customers, and we had to close down for a while until the manager came to fix it, and until the melted ice cream was wiped up from the floor.

The End of a Slippery Tale.

PART IX

THE CONVENT YEARS

After I graduated, I entered the Convent in 1953 at 18 years of age. I hadn't planned on being a nun; I was going to be an actress. However, God had other ideas for me, instead.

My mother was in the hospital after a serious operation; and when I saw her, I could tell that she was not going to live. After I left the hospital, I ran to the Church and went up to the Altar, and I knelt down and prayed, "God, if you let my mom live, I promise you I will enter the Convent. But I won't promise you I will stay." I didn't want to make a promise to God that I might not keep, so I just promised Him that I would enter, but not that I would stay.

The next day my mom got better, so I knew I had to keep my promise to God. (I never did tell my mother or father why I decided to become a nun. All I said was that I was going to enter the Convent.)

When my mother heard that I was going to be a nun she ran to the parish priest and said, "Father, my daughter wants to be a nun. He answered her, "What's wrong with that?" and she answered, "But Father, you don't know my daughter!" And he really didn't, but that didn't stop me from entering the Convent, even though it was the hardest thing for me to do.

But a promise is a promise, especially to God.

MY LAST NIGHT AT HOME

The last night before I left Utah, I was sitting with my boyfriend at the Drive-In Movie watching "Moulin Rouge." The
words to the theme song of the movie were: "Whenever we kiss,
I worry and wonder. You're close to me, dear but where is your
heart?" This song was so appropriate, as by the following week
my boyfriend would soon find out the answer to "where is your
heart?" and where my heart was going—and me, along with it.

As far as my boyfriend knew, my Speech/Drama teacher
was sending me to New York City to the School of Acting.
However, I never told him about the change in plans—that I was
going to New York, all right—but into the Convent. I never told
him nor any of my friends, as they were not of the Catholic faith
and I felt at the time that they would never understand (although
later on, I found out that they would have). So I decided to wait
until I was far gone and let my mother give them the news.

Knowing that this was my last night with my boyfriend, I
was going to make sure this night would be as good as it could
get by having a real out-and-out smooching time with my boyfriend—for tomorrow, I would be on that train heading for the
Convent. I just had to have one last fling. After all, from now on
there would be no more fling. That definitely would be taboo, as
nuns didn't date nor marry.

OOPS!
THE LAST TALE WAS NOT THE LAST FLING

The dreaded day came when it was time for me to leave my home, which at the time I thought was forever. However, it wasn't: I did get to go back home as a nun, fourteen years later.

The journey for me was clear across the United States—from Salt Lake City, Utah to the Convent Headquarters (known as the Mother-house) in Poughkeepsie, New York. Two of the Catholic Sisters drove me and my parents to the train station. I have to admit, it was so very painful for me to leave home. The force behind this was the Promise I had made to God, and I truly felt I had to honor it!

When the train pulled out, I cried all the way until I reached New York City, where I got off at Grand Central Station and changed to another train that would take me to my destination: Poughkeepsie, New York. I really can't remember the actual time we left Grand Central Station or how long it took to get to the final destination (after all, it was 62 years ago); but what I do remember is that when we reached Poughkeepsie, it was morning.

Now, on this train, I stopped crying--and you will soon find out why. After all these years, I have never forgotten this train ride to Poughkeepsie.

I was seated on the train sitting by the window when a real handsome soldier—and I mean *handsome*—came and sat right next to me. The Conductor came to our seat and checked out our tickets. And as he did so, he gave us a sly smile, as if he knew it was going to be a memorable trip for both of us.

The lights on the cars of the train were dimmed to make it more pleasant for those who wanted to sleep. Sleeping was not in the picture for this handsome soldier and me; we were immediately attracted to each other, and the sparks really started to fly. And so he cuddled up to me and I let him--he put his arm around me, and I let him--and then he started kissing me, and I let him. After all, I might as well have another—and this time for sure, the very last—fling.

It didn't seem to bother me that here I was, kissing a total stranger on the train, with others right around us and the Conductor passing by now and then to make sure everyone's needs were being met. Morning came, and the train arrived into the station at Poughkeepsie. And as I looked out the window of the train, I could see two nuns standing there on the platform, waiting for me.

As I was getting up, ready to leave, I didn't say anything to the soldier; I just said goodbye. And then, as I was walking to get off of the train, I turned to look at him for the last time, and I saw him slip over to where I had been sitting so that he could look out the window. When I reached the platform, the two nuns came over to me and greeted me, and so we left the station; and as we were leaving, I turned and looked one more time at the train.

Years later, this scene has come into my mind more than once—seeing this handsome soldier, whom I knew absolutely knowing about except that he was leaving for active duty in Korea. I often wondered what he thought when he saw me walking away from the station with me in the middle and two nuns on either side of me.

PROLOGUE TO THE NEXT SET OF TALES OF LIFE IN THE CONVENT: 1953 to 1978

Before I begin these tales, for those of you who are not familiar with the Catholic Church or the Catholic Sisters within the Church, I want to share this information with you.

There are different communities of Sisters. These communities are made up of what we call *Orders* of Sisters, meaning that women can join different Orders, such as the Franciscan Order, the Dominican Order, Sisters of Charity, etc. Each community of sisters has its own rules, regulations, forms of worship, and main field of service—such as Teachers, Nurses, Social Service Workers, Psychiatrists, etc.

Our community of Sisters was of the Franciscan Order, and our work was in Social Service and Religious Studies. Our work varied according to the location, the country, and the size of the town or city. Our calling was to serve and to help fulfill the needs of others in many areas of life. We worked with the poor, the marginalized, the elderly, the mentally challenged, and the disabled of all ages and in all walks of life. We had kindergartens and Childcare Centers, and in the big cities we had settlement houses, soup kitchens, counseling, etc. We were there for everyone, regardless of lifestyles, race, color, and creed. We never used our work to proselytize—our goal was to be there in caring and mercy, showing unconditional love to others free of judgment and partiality.

In the beginning of my life in the Convent in 1953, my Community was very austere and had rigid rules. However, when Pope John the 23rd was elected Pope of the Catholic Church, he mandated that all Communities of Sisters, ours included, change the strictness of lifestyles within the Convents and be updated to the present times. I must admit that I was absolutely delighted, as I always was a very independent person; so this suited me just fine. We still had rules that we had to keep, but it was much easier than before.

Before I go on any further with my tales, I want to say that out of respect for the Catholic Sisters (Nuns), for the Priests, Church Members, and people in the towns, I have not used real names of the people or the places where I actually was stationed as a Catholic Sister in the Church. The tales are being told primarily just to bring you a smile or hopefully even laughter, and thus take you away for a while into a new adventure in reading.

Needless to say, a whole new world was opening up to me--one that was so very different from what I thought it would be. I had not counted on the strictness, nor the austerity of the living quarters, nor the fact that we would be ruled not only by the Sisters in charge but also by the clock. Everything was timed: getting up in the morning at 5 AM, Meditation, Prayers, Mass in the Chapel, daily chores in the morning, then prayers in Chapel, then noon lunch, more prayers in the chapel, then classes, then an hour of recreation and classes, followed by more chores, prayers in chapel, supper, prayers, and night recreation.

When we first entered, we were called Postulants. We wore a long black dress and a cape over our shoulders, and a black veil for our heads with the front part of our hair showing from underneath the veil. Those of you who saw the musical "Sound of Music" saw the type of uniform that we wore and what we looked like as Postulants.

When we were working, we would wear a checkered apron over our dress. We were kept secluded from the other Sisters except for prayers, eating, and working and recreation. We were only allowed to talk to them when it was absolutely necessary. After nine months in training, those of who stayed on in the Community were then accepted into the Novitiate. At that time we would receive our uniform, which we called a Habit. It was just like the professed sisters habits, except that our veils were white and not black. Our lifestyle was just the same as when we were Postulants.

Our recreation at night (except for Holidays and Feast Days) consisted of knitting, crocheting, embroidering, or darning socks. For me, this definitely was *not* recreation. I always steered away from anything like that, growing up as a child. It didn't appeal to me at all. My mother finally gave up on me when it came to anything like needlework and sewing. She had even remarked to me that someday I would be sorry for not learning, after I had refused to put my hand to anything in the area of sewing, which I considered a pure waste of time—and here I was, having to do the very thing I detested, almost every single night. To me, this was not recreation; this was a huge penance.

Also, on the first day, I found out that silence was to be kept at all times, except for when we needed to talk for a specific reason. We were allowed to talk with each other during afternoon/evening recreation time. Our afternoon recreations (when it was good weather) consisted of walking through the grounds of wooded areas on a hillside. If the weather was inclement, or it was wintertime, then it would be board games in the community room. If it was a holiday or what we would call a Feast Day, then we would be able to talk at our meals; and at recreation, we could listen to music on a record player (no CD players in those early days) and play different types of games, both afternoons and evenings. And on special occasions, we got to see a movie that would be ordered and shown in the large recreation hall. We would also be in plays that would be put on for the Sisters of our community.

Those who know me today cannot believe that I could keep silent all that time. For them, that was a miracle in itself, because I love to talk, share stories, tell jokes, etc. I do have to admit, keeping silent, then, was very difficult for me.

POSTULANT AND NOVITIATE YEARS: 1953-1956

Tale # 1: My First Night in the Convent

That night, after our evening prayers, we all went to our own cells (bedrooms) for the night. Our cells consisted of a single bed, a stand that held a wash basin with a pitcher in it for morning and night ablutions, a chair at the end of the bed, and a high small window up over the bed.

I was extremely tired after the long trip of two nights and four days by train, as well as the excitement of being in a new place that was so unfamiliar to me. It didn't take me long to fall asleep after I got into bed that night. As I was sleeping, I was awakened by large booming sounds like gunfire or cannons coming from outside. My first thought was that we were being attacked by Korea, as we were at war with Korea at that time.

Fear permeated my whole body as I lay there trembling, waiting for the Convent to be hit by artillery, as I was sure we had been invaded by the Korean Army. The sounds were just the same as in the newsreels and the movies. I couldn't go to anyone to find out what was really going on, as it was forbidden to talk in the Great Silence and to enter anyone's cell. So I lay there with the covers over my head, shaking like a bowl of Jell-O.

Morning came, and all was quiet. Our Convent was still there, and I was okay. I had to wait until our Great Silence was broken before I could ask anyone what happened and if we were at war. The time of ordinary silence just seemed to take forever; but finally it was recreation time, and now I could talk.

I went over to the Novice Mistress and asked her, "Sister have we been invaded by Korea?" She looked at me with a quizzical look and then said; "For heaven's sakes child, no! What makes you ask such a question?" I replied: "All the artillery that was going off during the night." It was then that I found out that directly from our Convent across the Hudson River from us was West Point. They would often do their military practices during the night or early hours in the morning before daylight. All the others in the convent already knew and were aware about West Point and were not fazed in the least by the sounds of artillery coming across the river. Needless to say I was much relieved and happy at the news and thanked God I was still alive and well.

Tale # 2: There's a Man in the House

After our night prayers, all the Professed Sisters—those of us in training (Postulants and Novices)—kept what they called "The Great Silence." Keeping the Great Silence meant no loud noises and no talking whatsoever. If it was necessary to speak, both parties would get down on one knee and whisper to one another. We were told that this was to honor the Blessed Lord when He was laid in his Tomb. Looking back, I feel it was just a good way to keep us all silent and free of disturbances. Now mind you, I am sure I can be very wrong about this assumption.

To wake up the Professed Sisters in the Main Convent in the mornings, a Sister went from door to door, ringing a bell that she carried in her hand. On opening the door, as she was ringing the bell she would say in Latin, "Benedicamus Domino" ("Let us bless the Lord"), and each Sister would reply by saying, "Deo Gratias" ("Thanks be to God").

Very early one morning, it was an elderly Sister's turn to wake up the Professed Sisters. And as she started down the dark hallway to where the Sisters were sleeping, her foot bumped against something soft. She looked down, and there on the floor was a man sleeping! Usually, the doors were all locked at night, but for some reason the main door had not been checked to make sure it was locked. The homeless man, being inebriated, thought he was at the Saint Christopher's Inn, which housed Transients. This Inn was located halfway up the hill from the

Convent, and was taken care of by the Friars whose Monastery was on top of the hill.

The Sister—being terribly frightened by the man lying there on the floor, and realizing it was the time of the Great Silence—instead of screaming, went frantically from door to door. And as she opened each door and rang her bell, instead of saying, "Benedicamus Domino" ("Let us Bless the Lord"), she said, "There's a man in the house, there's a man in the house!" And all the sisters answered back, as usual, "Deo Gratias" ("Thanks be to God").

Tale # 3: Only for Choir

Another rule was that singing secular songs were strictly forbidden, unless they were songs that the Postulant and Novice Mistress would pick out for us to sing. Then we would sing these songs on special occasions during recreation time, or putting on a performance for the other Sisters in the Community.

We took turns every month doing different jobs in the various Convent buildings or outside on the Convent grounds. This particular month, it was my duty to work out side, sweeping the sidewalks and picking up any debris that might be around.

I had just entered the Convent a couple of months before, and so as I was outdoors sweeping away, I got caught up with all the beauty of the early morning. The sun was just creeping up over the Catskill Mountains, sending rays of sunshine over the grounds; the birds were singing in the trees; and the dew from the previous night's cool air sparkled like miniature diamonds on the bushes and flowers. It all just seemed like a magical world, and it was oh-so-beautiful that I just couldn't help myself—and like Sister Maria in the movie "The Sound of Music, " I broke out into song, singing, "Oh What a Beautiful Morning, Oh what a Beautiful Day."

As I was singing away, a loud, firm voice came from out of nowhere: "Save your voice for choir!" I turned and looked, and there at the open window on the second floor was the head of the Mother General, looking at me very disapprovingly as she slammed down the window.

The Postulant Mistress heard about my infraction of the rule on singing a secular song. The next morning, I was kneeling and kissing the floor after hearing the penance that was given to me for singing. I wish I could say that this was the *only* penance given to me, but it wasn't. Again, like Sister Maria, I spent so many times kissing the floor that I can say what she said in the movie: "I have to kiss the floor so many times that now when I see the Mistress coming, I get down and kiss the floor before she says anything." To that statement I say: Ditto!

Tale # 4: First Time Having Chapel Duty

As I mentioned before, our duties during working hours were varied from month to month. This month was my first time to help Sister Sacristan. That was not her real name; she was given the title "Sister Sacristan," as her job was setting up for the Church Services and taking care of the Church that was located on the Convent grounds. Sister was one woman who expected you to do everything right and follow her orders to a tee!

The Church was large, as it also was the place of worship for townspeople. On weekdays, we had our own small chapels in each building for Mass, daily prayers, and Meditation; and on Sundays we would attend the service in the large church. The Sisters would be upstairs in the balcony, where they could look down on the congregation of townspeople below, and also the main Altar where the Priest would say Mass.

Each month, one Postulant was given the assignment to help Sister Sacristan after the Sunday Mass in the church— putting away the vestments, the altar cloths, etc. This month was my first time to help her. Since it was my first time, she would go over everything with me so that I could learn the ins and outs of my duties, so to speak, in helping her.

This Sunday, when the Mass was over, I went up to the Altar where Sister was standing. When she saw me, she said, "Sister, bring me the extinguisher."

I asked, "The extinguisher?"

She replied, "Yes, bring me the extinguisher so I can put out these candles." I looked at the Altar. It was full of lit candles, four on either side of the tabernacle, which meant eight candles on the lower part of the Altar itself. There also were shelf-like tiers behind the Altar that also held lit candles. Then, on either side of the Altar on the floor, were huge circular candelabras on a stand. Each candelabrum held three tiers of candles, which also were lit.

As I looked at all these lighted candles, I asked her again, "You want me to bring you the extinguisher?" We always *blew out* the candles at home, so I did not have a clue as to what she meant by the "extinguisher."

She said to me, win a harsh, irritable voice, " Yes, bring me the extinguisher!"

Seeing all the lit candles, I thought to myself, *Yes, it does look dangerous. The hangings behind the altar could go up in flame any minute, now.* So I went into the room that we called the Sacristy, where we kept all the vestments, candles, and other equipment. I looked around and then saw the fire extinguisher hanging on a holder on the wall. Aha, I had found what she wanted. So I took it down from the wall and brought it to her.

As I got ready to hand it to her, she took one look at me with the fire extinguisher in my hand, and—with pure disdain on her face—said to me in a livid voice, "I'll get it myself—you Peterkin!"

Now, I don't know what that word meant; but I knew it

was not meant to be very complimentary—and maybe it is just as well that I didn't know what she meant. However, when I saw her return with the candle snuffer, I learned what she meant by "extinguisher." Amen to this tale! Amen!

Tale # 5: Oh, the Poor Bride!

As mentioned before, the church on the Convent grounds was primarily for the townspeople in the surrounding little villages. Like other churches, we also had weddings that were held in our church.

It was Friday morning, and another Postulant and I were told we had to help get the church ready for the wedding that would take place the following day. This wedding was going to be momentous, as many influential people would be attending the ceremony. The church needed to be cleaned and shiny from top to bottom.

That morning, we dusted all the pews and everything else in the small church, and made sure that the candelabras and candleholders were all shining. When we came back in the afternoon, after our lunch and Divine Office (prayers), there were two cans of wax, rags, and hand buffers waiting for us. We were told to wax the floor and polish it. Now mind you, we did this on our hands and knees. It took us the whole afternoon.

We had just finished when Sister Sacristan came in to check on us. She looked around and then gave her nod of approval, which made us very happy in spite of the fact that we both were really tired. She also was most pleased to see that we had correctly set the two chairs in the right place, in front of the altar, where the bride and groom would be sitting during the wedding ceremony.

Saturday came, and the wedding took place. We were not present for the wedding; only Sister Sacristan would be there to light the candles, etc. After the wedding, we came over to help Sister put everything back in place and sweep the rice off of the sidewalk outside. As we entered the church, Sister was standing there with a face that showed the expression of anger. She looked at the two of us, and in a very cold, angry voice, said, "Which one of you waxed the floor by the Altar?"

I replied, "I did, Sister."

She then said, "Wouldn't you guess it! I don't know what I am going to do with you!" Then, without stopping, she continued, "Why did we ever accept you in the first place? What you did was a terrible disgrace to me and to the whole community."

Now, I know you are wondering what I did that created such an angry response from Sister Sacristan. Well, I will tell you: after I had finished waxing the floor, unbeknownst to all I had left the lid of the empty wax can on the bride's chair; and when the bride rose up from her chair, with her back to the congregation, everyone could see the lid of the wax can stuck to her bottom on her beautiful wedding gown.

Tale # 6: Those Poor Friars

Every time we chanted our Divine Office, we would end with the "Our Father Prayer" and the Hail Mary, which all knew by heart. After saying these prayers, we would all pray in unison. And of course, I would be fervently saying this prayer with them: "Gather up the Friars that none of them be lost."

This prayer always had me puzzled, as I really didn't know what was wrong with the poor Friars. Was the fear that they might give into temptation, and then lose their souls forever in hell? Months later, I discovered what the sisters were really praying was: "Gather up the fragments that none be lost."

Tale # 7: Meditation "Over-Time"

Morning and evening, we would have Meditation for a half hour. Don't ask me why, but I cannot meditate, even to this day. I've read all the books on Meditation by Theologians, Philosophers, Saints, and Mystical Teachers, and I've heard many lectures, etc. on how to meditate; but for me, to no avail.

Now, in the Convent, our Meditation was always led by one of the Sisters reading from a book with a special theme for that day for us to meditate on. And when it was time to finish, the Sister would then end with a prayer, and then we would leave the Chapel.

On this one occasion, after the Sister who was leading us in Meditation finished reading to us and we began meditating, she must have either fallen asleep or had an out-of-body experience. All I know is that we were in there for a long time—in fact, so long—that I said to one of the Sisters afterwards, "Wow, the Meditation was so long, I even ran out of distractions."

Tale # 8: "I'm Going to Faint—I Can't Breathe"

It was my turn to polish the floor of the large hall. This was where we would put on plays for festive occasions, where guest speakers would address us, and where we took piano lessons and recreation.

I was busy running the heavy polisher over the waxed floor. When I came to the piano, I knew that it needed to be moved, as we were required to polish under it, as well. As I was moving the piano, I felt something happen inside of me. All of sudden, I had this pain in my back. I was really hurting, and yet I finished my job. I did not want to say anything to the Novice Mistress, as I was afraid of getting admonished and being given a penance for moving a heavy object by myself, as we were supposed to get help with moving such items.

I didn't know what to do, so I went and found my Sister companion, knowing I could confide in her without it going any further. I told her about my moving the heavy piano, and that I had hurt myself and didn't know what to do. She told me that when *her* back was hurting, she was taken to the doctor, and told to wear a girdle. She then said that she would lend me her girdle, as she was no longer wearing it. She went to her cell (that is what we called the room we slept in) and got her girdle, and secretly handed it to me. I went into the bathroom, slipped it on, and then went to Chapel with the other Sisters for prayer.

As I sat in Chapel, I could feel that the girdle was really

getting tighter on me. When Sister had given me her girdle, it hadn't dawned on me that she very thin and there was no way that her girdle would ever fit me. When I had gone to put it on, I had found myself pulling and tugging the girdle to try to get it on all the way. Not knowing any better, I thought that was the way it should be, and that it was natural to feel so restricted.

We were only halfway through our prayers in the Chapel, and the tightness of the girdle around my waist was gaining momentum. When the last prayer was over and we were walking out of the Chapel on our way to the dining room, I felt so miserable and trapped. But I did not want to miss supper, as I would have to give the Novice Mistress an explanation as to why, and then I would be in real trouble—first for moving the piano, and secondly for borrowing the girdle without first asking permission from the Novice Mistress.

I felt so constricted by the girdle that I could hardly eat at all, and so I left most of the food on my plate. This was a no-no, as we were supposed to eat everything the Novice Mistress put on our plates. I just looked at her (she always sat at the head of the table), and, placing my hand on my stomach, I gave the gesture that I was not feeling well.

When the meal was finished, we headed back to Chapel for evening prayer. By this time, the girdle had slipped up and was around my mid-section, which made me feel like I was being cut in half. And as we walked down the dark corridor, I pulled up the side of my habit and tugged on one side of the girdle until it came down in place, and then I did the same on the other side, as well. It provided some relief, but I was still in agony.

That evening, I was the Cantor. I introduced the psalm, and then I sat down with the rest of the Sisters to chant the psalm. As I sat down, I felt the girdle slip back up around my mid-waist, squeezing the air out of me. When it was time for me to stand up to introduce the next psalm, as I was rising up from the pew I tried to pull the girdle down through my habit, but to no avail. It just would not budge. During the next psalm, I was in such agony that I could hardly get my breath. I just felt that any minute, I was going to faint. I got up from the pew and headed down the aisle out of the Chapel. I knew I would have to give an explanation for why I left, but at this time, feeling like I was going to die, I couldn't care less.

I didn't know where to go to take off my girdle, as we were in the main building and were not allowed to go upstairs where the Professed Sisters had their rooms. So I ran downstairs (by the way, we were forbidden to run) to the laundry room, as I knew no one would be there—everyone was in chapel. I took the suffocating girdle off with a huge groan of relief. It was so good to be able to breathe normally again. Then I thought, *What am I going to do with it?* I could not go back into the Chapel carrying the girdle in my hands. Then I remembered the shelf-like boxes in the laundry room with our names on them for our own clothes to be put into after they were washed, dried, and folded. So I went to my Sister-friend's box and placed her girdle inside, knowing that no one would look there until laundry day. My plan was to let Sister know where her girdle was so she could pick it up before then.

I went back into Chapel, and this time I was praising God for a very different reason—that I had found relief from my personal torture chamber. After we left Chapel, I thought that our Novice Mistress would come over to me and ask me why I had left earlier. However, I was so surprised, as she didn't ask me—not then, nor during our recreational hour, nor on our way to the private Chapel for our own personal night prayers. I gave thanks to God again that she never asked me, and I felt so happy inside with the feeling that all was well.

As I was walking out of the Chapel, to my surprise the Novice Mistress had not gone to her cell but was standing there, waiting for me. Without one single word, she lifted her index finger with the gesture of "come hither and follow me." My heart dropped down to my feet. I was so scared, as I knew I would have to tell her the whole story—and then, retribution time. Yikes!

I followed the Mistress to her office, and as I was walking I was thinking of what and how I was going to tell her. I could tell her that I was sick, as that wouldn't be a lie—for the girdle had made me feel really miserable and ill. So now I had my reason for not eating all my food and for leaving Chapel, and I felt some relief.

When we went inside her office, she motioned to me to sit down in the chair facing where she would be sitting. I sat down, feeling my heart racing inside of me, waiting for the unwanted question. She looked me straight in my face and said; "Sister why did you not eat your meal, and why did you leave the Chapel?" I took a deep breath and, trying not to look at her face, I replied, "I was sick."

She gave me a stern look and then said, "Sister, you are not telling me the truth!"

I was so shocked. How did she *know* that I wasn't telling the whole truth—how did she know? My heart now was pounding so hard that I thought it was going to bounce right out of my chest.

But before I could answer her, she said to me, "Would you like me to tell you why I know you are not telling me the truth?"

I nodded my head "Yes," wondering what she was going to say to me.

"All right, Sister, I will tell you. It was because you were so upset at what I taught in our class today. You were upset because I was talking about sex, and telling you about what takes place between a man and a woman. You have to be aware of this, as you will be working out in the world, and also you will be taking the vow of Chastity. You need to learn all this so you will be prepared on how to conduct yourself when you are back out in the world. I can tell that this talk was too much for you and you were really upset over the class—am I not right, Sister?"

Mind you, it was the early 1950s, before the Sexual Revolution, and sex was taboo among most God-fearing parents. Something you never talked about. She figured we Postulants were very ignorant about the subject. I was so relieved that I didn't have to fess-up, even though I knew she was so very wrong in her thinking. I knew *all* about the subject. I had even taken a Home Nursing course my senior year in high school, where we learned all about conception, how to deliver a baby, etc. And of course sex was something we kids secretly talked about in our school years. So I was far from being ignorant on the subject.

However, rather than get into trouble, I let her believe that this was my problem. And with a smile on her face, she told me that she was sorry I was so upset about the class, and that she really did understand my being so stressed out about it. Then she gave me her blessing and, with a smile on her face, opened the door for me to leave.

Walking out of her office, I was laughing to myself over what she had told me, and feeling so good that I had gotten away with my misadventures. I was relieved and thanked God for saving me from getting into big trouble and being given a big penance.

And another good thing came out of that evening session: it was the very first time I ever experienced a moment of kindness from her. You can believe me, I was one very happy camper that night.

THE REFECTORY (DINING ROOM) DUTIES

Tale # 1: Oh, What Beautiful Snow

There were only two of us who had entered the Convent that September, so both of us were together a lot of the time. The Postulant Mistress was often quoted as saying that she had more trouble keeping track of the two of us than she had previously had with *twenty* Postulants.

The Mother House (where the Mother General and Professed Sisters lived) not only housed the Professed Sisters but also contained the Chapel, kitchen, and dining hall where everyone in the community would pray and eat.

In the evening, the Novices would go with the Professed Sisters to Chapel for prayer, called the "Divine Office," which left the other Sister and myself to do the dishes. We had to clear the wooden tables and scrub them with a brush so that they would be free from stains. There was a separate room with a large double sink, and long counters on either side for washing and drying the dishes. I and the other postulant would take turns doing the washing and drying.

This one evening, when we had finished our work and the Sisters were still at prayer, either the Sisters were longer in Chapel or we were faster in doing the dishes—I don't know which. But whatever the case, we were happy to be finished with our chores. We opened the kitchen door to get some fresh air; and as we looked out, we saw a blanket of fresh white snow on the ground. It was so pristine, and so inviting us to go outside. Even though it was dark, the large outside light lit up the area around the kitchen; so out we went. And looking at Mother Nature's lovely, soft canvas on the ground, we came up with the bright idea of making snow angels.

If you have never heard of making snow angels before, I will now explain to you how it is done. You fall down on your back on the snow, so as not to disturb the snow around you, and then you spread out your arms, not touching the snow. With each arm up in the air, starting at the top of your head you put both of your arms down in the snow and move your arms back and forth, up and down, to make angel wings. You then get up very carefully; and on Mother Nature's canvas, you have a lovely large angel figure in the snow.

So here were the two of us, lying on our backs in the snow, making snow angels. We were having so much fun that we didn't think of being caught in the act—but we were; and of all things, it was the head of our Community, the Mother General, who caught us. Looking at us she said, "Sisters must keep their religious decorum at all times." Then she walked away.

We thought for sure we would get a penance the next morning. And the next morning, standing around the large table after breakfast, with the Postulant Mistress standing at the top, we were so dreading that moment, and wished we could be anywhere than there. For we were certain we were going to be admonished and given a penance. It seemed forever for the Postulant Mistress to speak to us—and were we ever surprised and relieved! There was not one word about us making snow angels. She only gave us our duties for the day. We left that session full of inner joy and gratefulness, and yet puzzled that we did not get admonished for our snow angels.

Looking back, I feel that the Mother General must have been amused at the two of us having so much fun, and must have decided not to mention it to our Postulant Mistress. And I am most certain that all the Postulants before us and after us— even to this present day—never made snow angels.

Tale # 2: The Newly Built Mother House and the New Dishwasher

The new main building was now finished where the Mother General and Professed Sisters would live, and where all of us (Postulants and Novices) would have our meals and pray in the new Chapel. The huge laundry room was downstairs, where we all had to help out on laundry day, a Tuesday. (We Novices would call it "Stewsday," as that was the day the cook cleaned out the walk-in refrigerator and would make a stew out of the leftovers. Actually Tuesday, was not our favorite day at all.)

To me, the best thing about the new building was the new dishwashing machine. Oh, how great it was for us to have a dishwasher! After having to do dishes for the whole community by hand for about at least a year, it was such a blessing for us. It was a large, metal dishwasher, where you would open a sliding door on one side to put the dirty dishes in and on the other side, you would open another sliding door to take the clean dishes out. The dishes all had to be dried with dishtowels when they were taken out of the dishwasher.

Sister and I would clear the tables together; and then when we were finished, we would then take turns putting the dirty dishes into the dishwasher, and then drying the clean dish- es with a towel when they came out of the machine.

After the dishes had been washed and dried and put away, along with the pots and pans that we had washed and dried in the kitchen, we then had to wash all the dishtowels by hand and hang them up to dry. We would use many dishtowels, and the idea of having to wash all of them really was the pits for us; so we looked for a way to get out of having to wash them.

How did we do this? Well to get out of doing extra work, the two of us came up with a great idea (or so we thought) for washing the dishtowels: we would throw them in the dishwasher, and let it wash the towels for us. We could get away with this, as there was no one around to check on us; the Sisters were in Chapel, praying. We were so pleased and happy with ourselves for coming up with such a great idea. However, it wasn't very long after we conceived this unique way of washing towels that it backfired on us.

I don't remember how long we had been using this method of washing the towels. All I remember is that we were washing the dishes in the dishwasher—and all of a sudden, it started overflowing, and water was running out from it all over the place. We didn't know how to shut off the machine, but finally we found the valve to shut the water off.

We had no idea why that had happened. We hurried and got out the mops and wiped up the water from the floor and on the counters. We finished just in time before the head Sister of the kitchen and refectory duties (she was also the permanent cook) came back from prayer. At this point, we were washing and drying the dishes by hand. She asked us why we were not using the dishwasher; and so we told her that we did not know why, but the dishwasher had overflowed.

The next day she called the company that had sold the dishwasher to the Convent, and complained that the new dishwasher was defective and would someone please come out right away and either fix it or give us a new one. That day and night, we washed the dishes by hand again; and the next morning, the man from the company was there to check out the new, defective dishwasher.

The repairman was dumbfounded as to why the dishwasher was all plugged up. He just didn't know what to make of it. Since the two us were on Refectory duty for the month, we happened to be there setting up the tables in the Refectory for noon meal. We both were called into the room off the kitchen where the dishwasher was; and there, on the counter, were the inside parts of the dishwasher spread out, with the bewildered repairman standing beside them. Sister cook was there, as well; and since she was the one who had made the phone call, the repairman asked her if more than just dishes were being washed in the dishwasher.

My partner-in-crime and I looked at each other while Sister was answering the repairman's question. The Sister replied, "Of course not! We would never wash anything else but dishes in the machine." The repairman said, "If that is true, then tell me: where did all this lint come from that plugged up the drain pipe? I can't figure it out." Sister then turned to the two of us and asked, "Sisters, do you know the how of this question?"

We both nodded our heads "Yes," and fessed up to our having washed the towels in the dishwasher.

We both were 18 years of age, and maybe we should have known better. But we didn't; and from this experience, we learned that you don't wash dishtowels in the dishwasher. Needless to say we received a good penance for this misdeed. And with that, I will end this tale.

Tale # 3: Getting Caught Being Late

It was again my turn to work in the Refectory. I was a Novice by this time, and as I was leaving our building, one of the new Postulants came to me for help. Knowing that I would be late for my job if I stayed and helped her, still I knew that I just had to help her. For in my heart, I felt it was the Christian thing to do, even though it meant I would be late for Refectory duty. So I stayed and helped her, and then left for my own job, feeling very good about myself.

As I was walking to the main Convent, I heard a voice behind me call out, "Sister, come here." I turned around, and there was our Novice Mistress standing on the sidewalk a little ways behind me. I walked back to her, and as I stood there she gave me a stern look and said, "Where are you supposed to be at this time?"

I replied, "In the Refectory."

"You do realize you are late?" she asked.

I replied, "Yes," and then I told her the reason why I was late, all the while thinking she would be so pleased with me for doing a Christian act and tell me how very good it was of me to be so kind. Instead, I was given a penance of kissing the floor in the Refectory each time I entered and left it. Can you imagine how many times that floor got kissed in those two weeks? I'm sure there is a smooth spot in that floor, still to this day, from all the kissing I did for those two weeks.

Tale # 4: The Irish Sister Cook

I'll never forget my first assignment for Kitchen Duty. The Sister cook was from Ireland. Not only did she speak with a heavy brogue, but she also used words that I had never heard before, and I certainly didn't have a clue as to what they meant.

For example, when she told me to put the pots and pans in the press, I looked at her and said, "The Press?"

"Yes, Sister," she replied, "put them in the Press."

Still dumbfounded by the word "press," I said to her, "The Press? What is the Press?"

With a sigh of disgust, she came over to me, took the pots out of my hands, brought them over to the cupboard, and—opening the doors—placed the pots inside. Then she turned to me and said in a condescending voice, "This is the Press. This is where you put the pots and pans." Then, looking at me, she said, "Why in the world did they send you to help me?"

As if this was not bad enough, after we had finished putting everything away and cleaning the sink and counters, she turned to me and said, "Sister, go outside and bring me the twig!"

I looked at her and said, "The Twig?"

At which she replied, "Yes, the Twig. Bring me the Twig from outside!"

Again, I said, "You really want a twig?"

By this time, irritation showed on her face, and she said,

"For heaven's sake, go out and get me that Twig!"

Realizing that I had better go and do as she said, I went outside and started looking around for a twig. I finally found a nice-sized one on the lawn underneath the tree. I went over and picked it up and brought it to her.

But when I went to hand it to her, she looked at me with such disdain and said, "What is the matter with you? Why did you give me this stick? This is not what I want. I'll get it myself!" Off she went outside—and came back with a broom in her hands from beside the outside door. It was then that I knew that a "twig" meant a broom.

I also learned that the word "clock" meant your face, and not the clock on the wall, and that "biscuits" meant cookies. After I caught on to her terminology and learned all that was expected of me, we both got along very well. And when it was my turn to come back again for Kitchen Duty, I was always greeted with a big smile.

GETTING READY FOR
OUR FIRST PROFESSION
(Taking of Temporary Vows)

Two years had passed. Sister Mary and I had now completed all of our studies and training. The week before we were to make our first Profession and take our first vows as Professed Sisters in our Franciscan Community, we were to go on what was called a Retreat, where we would spend time in complete silence, prayer, and attending and listening to a Retreat Master, who was one of the priests from the monastery on the hill above us. He was to give us lectures twice a day on how to live a full religious life of prayer and work, and ways for us to nourish our souls through contemplation and prayer.

Sister Mary and I both found him very boring and dry. As he droned on and on...and on, sometimes it was hard for us to keep awake. I, for certain, would let my mind wander to greener pastures, so to speak.

During the Retreat, both Sister Mary and I came down with bronchitis, most likely due to the musty, damp place where our lectures were held. During the very last lecture of the last day of our Retreat, Sister and I could not stop coughing. It was like an echo of coughs: first one of us would cough, and then the other. So the Retreat Master would stop lecturing, then wait for us to stop coughing, and then he'd go on with his lecture.

After a while, with the constant coughing from both of us, he finally could not take it any longer. In a loud, angry voice, he said, "When the Mother General told me that they were accepting two more Sisters into the ranks, she didn't tell me that the Community was accepting physical wrecks!" With this, he got up from his chair and stomped out of the room, slamming the door behind him.

PART X

PHASE 2: CONVENT LIFE ON THE MISSIONS

After we finished training and had taken our Vows of Chastity, Poverty, and Obedience, we were then sent out to places we called our Missions. We were Social Service Workers. As I mentioned before, we worked in the community. Wherever there was a need, we would be there to serve in any way we could to help make life better—to help in any way we could. We were there for everyone, regardless of race, color, or creed. We held everyone in great respect, regardless of their position or station in life. We just wanted them to know that we loved and cared about them, with no strings attached.

We also were Catechetical (Taught Religion) Teachers for those of the Catholic faith or those who would be interested in Religious Studies. Our Services as Social Service Workers would be varied, depending on where our Convents were stationed in the large cities, smaller cities and towns, or foreign lands. All in all, we were there to SERVE!

Tale # 1: My First Mission

I had just turned 20 years of age when I went to my first mission in September of 1955. The mission was in a mining town in Upper New York State. It was located right on the Canadian border, not far from Montreal, Canada. Our Convent was on a top of a small hill; and right in the back of the Convent was the cemetery. You could actually say it was right in our backyard. At first, I did not feel good about looking out on gravestones as our landscape, and I did not like being out there after dark.

On the left side of the Convent was the Church, and on the right side of the Convent was one single home with a young couple, their three-year-old daughter, and the husband's father living there. Except for the Priest's residence on the other side of the Church, these were the only buildings. There were no homes or buildings below the hill, so we were quite secluded from the rest of the town. However, the town was within walking distance, and you could see it from where we were on top of the hill. Below us was a lovely small lake on one side of the road, and the woods on the other side of the road. There were four of us stationed there, one being our Superior. She took her job very seriously in letting us know who was in charge and that she would not take any nonsense from us.

I soon became acquainted with the family next door. The little three-year-old girl was so pretty, and precocious as well. Her mother, who I thought looked like the movie star Maureen

O'Hara, did not waste any time in letting me know of her displeasure at the grandfather's drinking so much. She said she would go through the home and find his whiskey bottles hidden in the dirty-laundry basket, behind the toilet, out in the garden, etc.—and she found this so frustrating, as she was trying to stop him from drinking. On top of it all, she could not find out how he was getting his whiskey, as he never left the place unless either she or her husband went with him; and when Grandpa did go with them, they kept a tight reign on him to make certain that he did not buy any whiskey when they were not looking.

I could have told her where he got his bottles, but I kept my mouth shut as I felt it was not up to me. I really liked the old guy and did not want to tattle on him, nor did I want to tell her how a friend of his was bringing the bottles and putting them in the mailbox. I happened, one day, to be looking out of the Convent window when I saw his friend place the bottle in the mailbox. (The mailboxes were on posts, like the ones in Charlie Brown comic strips where he is waiting for a card or letter from the little girl who stole his heart.) The mailboxes were down the road from the Convent and hidden from the grandfather's house, so no one except we Sisters could see them. A short time later, Grandpa would head down to the mailbox, take the whiskey out of the box, put it inside his shirt, and then head for home to look for a place to hide his whiskey once he got back to his house.

The Convent was a nice house, just like a family home. The only difference was that one room downstairs was a place of worship, called the Chapel. The upstairs had five bedrooms, and one large room we called our Community Room. My bedroom was the corner bedroom, and its windows looked out on the graveyard. At first, I really did not like having this as my last vision before I crawled into bed at night. For a while, looking out at the gravestones really spooked me.

This one evening, as I was sleeping, all of a sudden I was awakened by awful moaning and crying sounds coming from the cemetery. I thought to myself as I lay in bed, trembling from fright, *All those ghost stories are true after all—the dead do come back to life as ghosts.* The moaning and cries kept going on for what to me seemed endlessly. I wondered if the other Sisters were as frightened as I was. However, I was too frightened to even get out of bed. Finally, the noises stopped and I fell fast asleep.

The next morning, I asked the Sisters if they too had heard the screaming and moaning. They looked at each other and then smiled at me. It was then that I found out that when Grandpa would be well drunk, at times he would go into the cemetery and hide behind one of the large gravestones and just start making these awful eerie sounds, until his son came and got him and brought him back to the house.

End of my Ghost Story.

Tale # 2: Be Careful What You Do in the Cemetery

It was late fall, with a crispy-cold nip in the air—so much so that at times you could even see your own breath, it was that cold. This one Monday it happened to be a holiday, and when we had holidays we loved to take advantage by going to the small city to spend the day.

It just so happened that on this holiday, I had come down with the flu; and of course, I decided to stay home in bed. That early afternoon, I heard the front door bell ringing and ringing. I really didn't feel like going downstairs to answer the door. At the end of the long hallway was a window where you could look out and see the small porch below that led to the front door. With the doorbell still ringing, I got up out of bed and went to the window in the hallway and looked down on the small porch, and saw three of my fourth-grade boys standing there. After another long ring, I heard one of the boys say, "Good, no one's home!" Hearing this, I knew that they were up to some mischief.

I watched them as they walked away from the Convent and headed for the cemetery. My bedroom was right on that corner of the Convent where I could look out onto the cemetery, so I went over to the window and looked out. I saw the boys crouching down behind the very large family tombstone. *Hmm,* I said to myself, *I wonder what they are up to behind there.* So I stood there at the window, waiting and wondering what they were doing. Just then, white smoke started rising up from behind the tomb. The mystery was solved: they were smoking.

The next week in Religion Class, I looked at my three boys and said, "You have to be careful what you do in the cemetery. There were names of three boys on the Kowalowski tombstone saying these boys were smoking—and just like a puff of smoke, before I could read the names, they disappeared right before my eyes." The expressions on the boys' faces were classic. With large eyes, they looked at each other, and I could see how scared they were.

Yes, I know what you are thinking: "A nun, and she told a lie!" Do you really think it was wrong of me? And if so, do you think I will be forgiven? Anyway, I hope so. I was just 21 at the time. Does that exonerate me?

MORE TALES AS A SISTER
IN OTHER PARISHES

Tale # 1: It's In the Eyes of the Beholder!

*It was fall when I was sent to a new Parish, at 35 years of age.
There were only two of us Sisters there, the Superior and yours
truly.*

*It didn't take me long to become adjusted to my new as-
signment and to establish a relationship with members of our
church and people within the community. The youth in our
church took to me right away. I never did have any problem in
that regard—it may well be because they likened me to Sister
Maria in the movie, "The Sound of Music." In fact, grown-ups
as well as kids in the towns where I worked would tell me, "Oh,
you are just like Sister Maria in the movie." During the time of
the TV show "The Flying Nun," children also called me "Sister
Bertrille," as well. Now, having said this, there may also have
been some adults, unbeknownst to me, who did not take to me. In
fact, I remember two such women in the Parish who didn't like
me at all; and this is the subject of this tale.*

After I had been in the Parish a few months, a woman who had
volunteered to be my helper with projects came to me and said,
"Well, Sister, it looks like we are going to have to keep you after
all."

I was very puzzled at her remark and asked her, "What do you mean?"

To which she replied, "Oh, the two elderly ladies—you know the ones I'm talking about—they went around and took up a petition to get you out of the Parish. And sorry to say, no one would sign it."

The two of us were really close friends, and we started to laugh. We both knew those two women so well. They had also taken up a petition against the Pastor: he'd had two trees removed from the grounds because of safety issues, and the ladies were very upset about it. It was no mystery to me why these two women wanted me out of the Parish. They had already let it be known to me that I did not meet their standards of a Catholic Sister, and felt that I was lacking in religious decorum. They could not accept my playing ball in the streets with the young kids; or driving around with my 10th-grade girls in an old beat-up truck with us laughing, singing, and having a great time; or jumping rope with the kids out in front of the Parish hall. The two ladies were there in the church to make sure that it met their standards for what the church, as well as those of us working in it, should be.

This brings to mind another incident regarding these two ladies. But before I go on any further, I must give you some background for my tale so that its ending will bring the punch of humor that I am seeking.

I am sure that you have heard how Catholics are known for "Catholic Guilt." When I took classes in Clinical Psychology, the professor posed to us this question: "I know religion can be very helpful to the mental health of people, yet at the same time I wonder if it cannot also be detrimental to mental health?" This question remained in my mind; and after much pondering, I became determined to eradicate "Catholic Guilt" as much as possible.

The school year started, and religion classes were starting, as well. I had the junior high (middle school) religion class. The first section of the class was geared to helping the students know the difference between what was a "real" sin and what wasn't– in other words, to helping them form their own conscience in order to eliminate "Catholic Guilt." Anyway, that was my objective. So I decided to start with our emotions.

I explained to the class that having feelings of jealousy and anger were not sins; that these emotions are just as much a part of us as sorrow, happiness, and love. Then I would give them an example of what I was talking about, to help them better understand that these emotions were not sinful, and that what matters is how we *handle* these feelings. I decided to use myself in this demonstration. I started by telling my students that being a Sister did not necessarily mean that I was holy or free from doing wrong—that, just like them I too had to work at trying to follow the precepts of God.

So, using myself to illustrate the subject of jealousy and

anger, I started with the emotion of jealousy. I told the class that I had felt very jealous when I was sent to a new Parish and I kept hearing about this wonderful Sister whose place I was taking. People kept telling me how wonderful she was, and how great she was at whatever task she was doing, how they missed her, etc., so feelings of jealousy rose up very strongly within me. I explained that having these feelings did not mean that I had sinned; this was just my emotion working inside of me. Then I told them that I *could* have sinned by using this emotion of jealousy in a wrong way—such as trying to destroy her reputation in the eyes of others by telling lies about her, or by saying something about her that I knew would lessen her in their eyes. In that case, yes, this would be sinful.

Then I went on to anger. I proceeded to tell the class that I had not handled the feeling of anger in the right way. I had gotten very angry at what the Pastor had said to me as I was putting the chairs away in the Parish hall, and in my anger I started to slam the chairs together and then slam them against the wall. So I told the class that I did not use my anger in the right way, as I could have damaged the chairs and the wall, and it was their parents' money that bought the chairs and paid for the paint for the walls; and thus I did not use my feelings of anger in the right way.

When I finished this class, the students left; and as I was leaving my classroom and was at the door to start down the hallway, I could hear the voices of the two women who wanted me out of the Parish coming from around the corner. They could not see me, nor could I see them, so I just stopped in my tracks to listen to the conversation they were having with some of the girls from my class.

I heard them ask the girls if they were just out of Religion class, and the girls in unison answered, "Yes." Then one of the women asked them who was their teacher, and they answered; "Sister Eloise!" Then the lady asked them, "Do you like her?" to which they replied, "Yeah she's great! She can sin just like the rest of us!"

Tale # 2: Just One Missing Letter

In one Parish I was, you could say, a "Jack of all trades," as I had many different jobs that I took on; and I enjoyed doing most of them. One job was out of necessity: the Church did not have a secretary, nor could they afford to hire one, so yours truly took on the task.

One of the weekly tasks was doing the Sunday bulletin, which would be passed out to the people leaving the Church after the services. These bulletins would list the up-coming week's events being held at the Church, as well as other information that would be pertinent to the Parishioners, along with the weekly and Sunday Mass schedule.

In the Catholic Church, besides the Sunday Mass (church service) there also is a Saturday evening Mass (the same as the Sunday Mass), which meant that the Sunday bulletin had to be ready for our Saturday- night Mass at 5 PM.

On Saturdays I worked most of the day at the town's Senior Center. I would try to leave early so that I would have the time to type the Sunday bulletin. Typing the bulletin was not an easy process, as we had manual typewriters (electric typewriters and computers were not invented as yet), which meant that printing the typed material was not so easy, either.

I'm sure some of you may not know what was involved in typing, in those days, or in making copies of what you had typed. First, the typewriter: before you started typing the bulletin, you would first place in the roller of the typewriter a waxy stencil, which you would type on. You had to hit the typewriter keys very hard so that the letters on the keyboard would cut through the waxy stencil. If you made an error, you had a small bottle with a wee wand in it, and you would dip the wand into a thick blue paint-like mixture. Then you would apply this mixture onto the wrong letter or word on the stencil, wait for it to dry, and then you would strike the key again, this time with the right letter. After that was all done, you would take your stencil and put it on a large round drum, which was part of the printing machine. You would have to be most careful when doing this; for if you pulled too tightly, you could tear the stencil, and then you would have to do the whole process all over again. Once the stencil was placed on the drum, you would turn the large handle on the drum over and over again until you were sure that the ink was even and would go through the letters on the stencil. You then would place the paper in the area on the drum provided that purpose, and then start turning the handle again. This time, the paper would slip through and come out at the other end with the printed material on the papers. After the ink dried, you would fold the sheet of paper in half. And that would be your Sunday bulletin.

On this one weekend, I was working late at the Senior Center, which I and another woman had started for the community. Suddenly, I remembered that I had not done the bulletin for Saturday and Sunday Mass. I hurried home, typed up the stencil, and ran it off on the printing machine. Then I hurried over to the Church and placed the copies of the bulletins on the table in the entrance of the Church. The church service had just started. I gave a sigh of relief as I left the bulletins on the table ready for the ushers to hand out to the parishioners as they were leaving the church.

After the 11:00 a.m. Sunday Mass the next day, I was standing at the entrance of the Church when I was approached by one of the men in our Parish, Mr. Smith. Knowing that I typed the bulletins, he said to me, "Sister, I always wondered what you thought of our Pastor. Now I know."

"What do you mean?" I asked.

He replied, "Don't you proofread your bulletin before you print it?"

I replied that I usually do, but this time I was so rushed to get the bulletins into the Church on time that I didn't have time to do it.

He then said to me, "Well, look at the weekday Masses and you will know what I am talking about." Then he walked away with a large grin on his face.

In the Catholic Church, we have daily Mass as well, and in the bulletins there is always a section for the Daily masses. For example: "Monday 8:00 am – Mary Drew / Tuesday 8:00 am – Special Intention Margaret Smith" – and so on for the rest of the weekday Masses.

After Mr. Smith walked away, I hurried and picked up a

bulletin. When I opened it, I went straight to the weekday Masses—and when I came to Wednesday, I noticed that I had left the "M" off "Mass." And this is how it read:

"Wednesday - There will be no <u>ass</u> in the church today as the Priest will be out of town."

ATTENDING THE UNIVERSITY
IN THE SUMMER TIME

Tale # 1: Oh My, How Embarrassing!

One summer, when I was in my thirties and attending Oregon State University, in Corvallis, Oregon, I had a wonderful experience when taking the Anthropology class. I loved Anthropology, and would take every course in that subject that was offered. This summer, our professor asked us to adopt some students on campus from another country so that we could learn all about their history, customs, lifestyles, etc., and really spend all the time we could with them, both day and night. This was for the full summer course, from June to September. (Sleeping with them was not advised.)

In the dorm where I stayed on campus, there were Japanese teachers from Japan who were living there, as well. They were at OSU taking English courses so that they could perfect their ability to teach English Courses in the schools when they returned to Japan. They happened to have their rooms on the same floor as I was on, and we had already been greeting each other and having a few chats together.

Out of the group of Japanese teachers, six of them always spent time together; you would hardly ever see them without all of them being together. One day, seeing them waiting for the elevator, I approached them and asked if I could meet with them in the lounge on our floor; and since I was no stranger to them, they felt comfortable agreeing to meet with me.

We met together that evening, and I explained to them what our professor had asked of us, and that I would so love it if I could belong to their group. And so the teachers graciously accepted me into their fold. I joined them in going to their classes; we went shopping together; we were together at recreation time, in many forms; and we had our meals together. It was not very long before we became very close friends and shared many, many happy times together. In fact, even after our summer session ended and they had returned to Japan, we kept in touch with each other. To this day, I think so lovingly about my wonderful friends and the time we spent together.

Before I finish this tale, I would like to mention an item that, for us, would be amusing but was very frustrating for my dear friends from Japan. During this era, the United States was importing most of its commodities and goods from Japan. When it came near the time for my dear friends to go back to their own country, they came to me very frustrated and upset. They had been out all day shopping, looking for souvenirs to bring back to their homeland with them; however, they came home empty-handed. I hadn't gone shopping with them, as I was studying for a final exam. When they came back they said to me in an unhappy voice, "We spent all day shopping to buy affordable gifts as souvenirs from America to bring back home for our families, but all the gifts are made in Japan."

Now back to my tale:

If I hadn't told my friends that I was a Catholic Sister, they certainly would not have known it. After years of wearing the traditional habit, by this time we Sisters had the choice of wearing secular clothes when we were away from our Parish. I chose to do so, as I wanted be looked upon by the professors as a student, and not as a Catholic Sister, so I could experience what it would be like as a regular student. Most of the time, I wore slacks and blouses. I must admit, I had a nice shape then (not anymore—far from it), and sometimes I would get a wolf call or whistle from a man on campus. I would smile to myself, thinking, *Wouldn't they be shocked to find out that I was a nun— or would they?* You will soon find out my reason for my telling you about wearing secular clothes.

Since my new Japanese friends and I frequently ate our meals together, I was able to introduce them to some of foods they had never tried before; and they always seemed to enjoy the experience. Most of the time, we would eat our meals together in the dinning hall on campus, called the MU building. The meals were cafeteria-style and actually were really delicious.

One time, there were only two of us for our evening meal—me and one of the men, whose name was Ichiro. I just loved cafeteria-style eating, as I could choose what I wanted or didn't want to eat. Ichiro and I filled up our plates. Then, placing them on trays, we went to find a table. All were taken except for one large round table. Being the very kind gentleman that he was, he proceeded to pull out my chair for me. So I sat down, and then he took his seat right across from me at the round table.

The cafeteria was full of people, which made it very noisy, and the talking was very loud. Sitting so far across from my friend made it very hard for me to hear him when he was speaking, as his voice was very low and soft. So in order to hear him better, I leaned over the table so I could be closer to him while he was talking, as I didn't want to make him feel uncomfortable by continually asking him to repeat what he was saying to me. I was responding to one of his comments—and as I was talking and leaning over the table, I could see that he really wanted to break out laughing; he was working so hard to keep a straight face. I wondered what I was saying that struck him as so funny. Then I followed where his eyes were looking—and as I did so, I looked down at my plate, where he was looking. There, resting in my heap of mashed potatoes, were my two boobs. When I sat up straight from bending over the table, there were my breasts, full of mashed potatoes, looking like two mountain peaks with snowcaps on them. I was so embarrassed that I just jumped up from my chair and said, "Oh, please excuse me!" and ran to the restroom to clean myself off.

Needless to say, I did not return to finish my meal.

Tale # 2: If They Only Knew

This tale takes place at a different university that I was attending. I will tell it without naming the university in order not to compromise anyone.

This university that I was attending was a very progressive one. I wanted to attend it one summer, as it offered me subjects that would help me in my field and the work towards my degree. One of the classes I was taking was a Sociology class titled "Aspects of Womanhood." I was always on the bandwagon for Woman's Lib, at that time, and so I felt that this course would contribute greatly to my working for that issue.

The first day in class was a real eye-opener for me. Even with my being a nun working in Social Service work and Counseling, I thought I knew pretty much of what went on in people's lives—or should I say, the sexual aspect of their lives. The class was small—perhaps12 to 14 of us women in the class. While I was at this university, as well, I wore secular clothes and I did not make it known that I was a nun. Which really turned out for the best, in this class.

The first day of class, the women shared their sexual lives and activities associated with it very openly, and what they liked in love making and what they didn't, leaving nothing to the imagination. Needless to say, I was most silent and didn't contribute to the general discussion for the whole time I was in that class. Actually, the classes were repetitious from that day on.

I was, and still am, a very open and friendly person, and never seemed to have any problems with people not liking me or wanting to distance themselves from me. Now mind you, I could be naive about this but I really don't think so, based on past life experience. However, for the first couple of weeks in this class, I was totally ignored. I felt the isolation like ice, not only from the women in the class but from the woman professor, as well. I tried to figure out what was wrong with me: Was it that I was not contributing to the conversations (as the class was more a discussion class than a lecture)? Or had they guessed my identity? Whatever the case, I was bothered by their exclusion of me.

After two or three weeks, the professor asked us to introduce ourselves, tell the class something about ourselves. Wow! I had a sickening feeling come over me. After hearing all that had been said in the classroom discussions, how could I ever tell them that I was a nun? I didn't want to make them feel uncomfortable or embarrass them in any way, and it also was very difficult for me to let them know I was a nun. As it got closer for me to introduce myself, I started to panic; and I prayed, "Oh dear God, please help me. I don't know what to tell the class."

Just then, I had a great idea about what to say to them. I would say something that was absolutely true: that I was the Director of the Senior Center in Wyoming—whew, thank the dear Lord I was saved from my dilemma!—and when the professor called on me, I told them about my position in Wyoming.

There was a huge reaction from the group. I was surprised that what I had said should cause this phenomenon in the classroom. Then one woman, who was like a leader of the group, said to me, "Do you know who we thought you were?"

Panic time again. I was sure they were going to say to me, "We thought you were a Catholic Nun" – and hesitantly, I said, "No I don't know."

Then she said to me, "We thought you were one of those rich dames up in the hills who would lounge by their pool, drinking martinis every day. You surprised us!"

From that day on, I was accepted and taken into the group as one of them. Even the professor warmed up to me. Oh, if they only knew. . . .

And another tale about that same class:

It was the Monday of the last week in class, and the professor told us that for the final grade we were to do a paper—to be read in class—about "Our Sexuality." She wanted us to write about our own sexual feelings, or we could even write about our experiences in that regard.

Oh my! When I heard what we were going to be graded on, I was really distressed. I couldn't figure out how I was ever going to do this. Should I not come to class that week? Or, worse yet, should I fess up and let the professor and the class know that I was a nun?

Needless to say, that night when I went home, I was beside myself—just couldn't concentrate on anything—even my always-ready appetite had diminished to zero. If I left class or if I came to class without a paper, I could be looking at an "Incomplete" or "Failure grade"! I didn't want that, as I did have a high average and I surely didn't want to jeopardize it—especially with only a year to go before I would graduate.

That evening, I decided that if I took a good shower before I went to bed, maybe—just maybe—it would help me to relax and, hopefully, fall asleep. I turned on the faucets in the shower to get the water to the right temperature; and when I was satisfied that the water was just right, I got into the shower.

Who would ever believe that this shower would be my salvation, and the answer to my prayer?

As I was showering, I came up with a brilliant idea—and I was ecstatic. I decided that I would do my paper about my shower! And since by this time I really can't remember exactly how I wrote it and I don't have a copy (the professor kept it), I will do my best to give you an idea of how I wrote my paper:

"What better way to get in touch with your sexuality and sensual feeling than to take a shower. To feel the warmth of the water as it gently falls upon your body, and the sensation of the soap as it touches your skin and as your body feels your hand with the soft-slippery motion as you wash yourself, along with the fragrance of the soap that reaches your nostrils and enlivens your senses, and as you step out of the shower feeling the warm softness of the towel as it touches your flesh while you are drying your body."

Of course, the paper was much longer and more descriptive. However, thanks to the dear Lord, I had my answer, and I could finish my course.

That Friday, when it came my turn to stand up and read my paper out loud, was I ever surprised at the reaction of the teacher and the women in the class. My paper was received with excessive praise and admiration, and all wanted a copy of it. Needless to say, I was dumbfounded and pleased at the same time. I never thought I would get so much adulation for my paper. I ended the course with an A+. I wonder what would they think if they ever found out I was a nun.

CHURCH SUMMER SCHOOL: OH, YUK-YUK!

Depending on where we were stationed in the summer time, we would hold Summer School for our Catholic grade-school kids. It would be held for two weeks, and on the last day we would give the children a party.

This one summer, we were given a large—and I mean *large*—amount of powdered milk. Our Superior decided that we would use it up by making hot chocolate for the children's party at the end of Summer School. She herself made the hot chocolate. However, in order to keep the powdered milk from sticking to the bottom of the humongously large pot, you had to continually stir it so that it would not burn. Sister Superior got tired of stirring the hot chocolate, so she told me to stir it for a while. She then left the kitchen.

I was doing just as she told me. I kept stirring and stirring and stirring the pot, and praying that she would soon come back so I could stop. When she came, she asked me if I had done as I was told and I said, "Yes, I did." She then she took the spoon from my hand, dipped it into the hot chocolate, and, taking the spoon out, sipped the hot chocolate. Then, with an angry look on her face, she said to me, "I thought you said you constantly stirred the hot chocolate. But you couldn't have, as this chocolate is burnt and doesn't taste a bit good!" I told her that I *did* keep stirring it; but she really didn't believe me and said to me, "I'm leaving for a while. And you had better see to it that all of this hot chocolate is gone, or else you are going to be in big trouble!" With that, she walked out the door.

Well, I realized what had happened to the chocolate. When I was stirring the hot chocolate, I didn't put the spoon far enough down to keep the powdered milk that we used in the chocolate drink from sticking to the bottom of the pan. Now, my challenge was to get rid of all this chocolate, as I did not want to get into trouble.

I thought to myself, *Well, the kids won't know the difference. They will drink it.* I went into the hall and had the kids all sit down at the table, which was already set with paper plates and paper cups. After the children were seated and we said Grace, I went and filled the pitcher full of hot chocolate and proceeded to fill their cups. As the children started to drink their chocolate, I heard these comments: "Yuk, this is awful!" "Phew, this stinks and tastes bad!" Another child said, "It don't look good and it don't taste good, I don't want it." All the other kids were in agreement with him.

I thought to myself, *Oh, what am I going to do? I just have to get rid of this hot chocolate.* Then an idea came to my mind: I remembered that I had a lovely picture of Jesus in a golden frame, a leftover from the prizes we had given to the children. So I called for quiet and attention, then I picked up the picture and asked, "Who would love to have this beautiful picture of Jesus?" All hands went up, and I said, "Okay, the first one who is finished with the chocolate drink, raise your hand

and you will get the prize." Immediately, the children picked up their cups and—holding their noses so they would lose some of the taste—drank their chocolate right down. The prize was given, and I was one happy nun, as all of the chocolate was gone.

UPSTATE NEW YORK

Tale # 1: Dear Aunt Rosy

In the 1950s (I was in my twenties, then), we Sisters were still living a strict life. (Our lifestyle changed in the middle 1960s to be more in tune with the times.) We were not allowed to eat with our family members or friends. If we served them lunch or snacks, we would do so in the living room of the Convent, and we would sit and visit with them while they ate; but we would not eat with them. If anyone came to the Convent during meal time, the Sister who had finished first or was the closest to being finished with her meal would be the one to go to the door. There were five of us in that Convent.

Now to Aunt Rosy: her real name was Rose but she wanted us to call her Aunt Rosy, as she was older than us except for Sister Agatha. Aunt Rosy would come every Saturday evening to the Convent to visit with us. She would give us an account of her weekly laundry: how she would wash the clothes—hers, her son's, and her two young grandsons'. Her son and his wife had divorced, so he had come back home with his two sons to live with his mom.

One part of this laundry wash list was disturbing to us: Aunt Rosy would tell us how she would also starch her son's and grandsons' underwear, shirts, pants, and pajamas. The first time she told us this, we asked her why she starched their clothes, as it would be most uncomfortable for them to wear not only during the day but to sleep in as well. Her reply was, "Well, if any one of them got in an accident or got ill and had to go to the Emergency Room, when they would strip them down, I want their underclothes or pajamas to look fresh and clean." We were all grateful that Aunt Rosy did not wash *our* clothes.

Tale # 2: Aunt Rosy's Pies

What we did love about Aunt Rosy coming over on Saturday nights was that she made the best apple pies we ever tasted, and I can say even to this day I have not had an apple pie that tasted as good as Aunt Rosy's. She would always send her son over to the Convent with the apple pie before our evening meal so that we could have her pie for desert. Then when she came, she would ask us how we enjoyed her pie, and we would honestly tell her how much we loved it.

One Saturday, for some unknown reason our Superior decided to bake a pie, as well. Could it be that she was a little jealous of Aunt Rosy's pies, hmmm, I wonder? Sister Superior was busy in the kitchen preparing our supper (we were supposed to take turns but, much to our dismay, she cooked most of the time), which—like most of the time—was spaghetti with no sauce, just olive oil poured over it. She was not a good cook, believe me! Then Sister Ann came into the kitchen carrying another pie that someone had brought, and placed it next to our Superior's pie on the counter. Now we had *two* pies for supper.

I had been gone for the day and had just come back. I went into the kitchen—and there I saw the two pies on the counter. As I looked at them I was so happy to see that one of them was a berry pie, and the other a banana cream pie that the Superior had made—and I thought to myself, *Okay, with Aunt Rosy's apple pie and these two pies, we are going to have a nice variety of pies*. And did that ever suit me to a "T": having those good pies would help to make up for our having to eat the Superior's cooking—you could say, they were like a reward. Just then, the doorbell rang and my Superior had me go to the door. We both knew for certain by looking at the clock that it would be Aunt Rosy's son with her delicious apple pie.

Sure enough, we were right. I took the pie from him, thanked him for bringing it, graciously said goodbye, and headed for the kitchen with the pie. When the Superior saw that it was Aunt Rosy's pie, she proceeded to tell me that we would be eating her own pie that night, and to take Aunt Rosy's pie along with the berry pie and put them in the freezer, downstairs in the basement.

That evening when the doorbell rang during our meal, since I had finished eating, the Superior had me go to the front door and stay with Aunt Rosy until the Sisters would join us. So I went to the front door and let Aunt Rosy in; and after she was seated, Aunt Rosy asked the question she always asked every time she came: "Sister, how did you like my apple pie?"

Knowing that we hadn't eaten her pie, and also knowing that she would be greatly hurt that we did not eat her pie that evening, I said a silent prayer, Dea*r God please forgive me for lying*. Than I proceeded to say to her, "Oh, Aunt Rosy, your pie was absolutely delicious."

"You really did like it, then?" she asked.

"Oh yes," I replied.

"Are you sure you really did like my pie?" she asked again. (This kind of conversation was not unusual. This was the way it went every time she came.)

"Oh Aunt Rosy," I said, "it was the best pie that you ever made. It was so delicious."

Then she asked me, "You sisters *did* put the pie in the oven like I told you?"

To which I answered, "Oh no, we ate it just like it was."

Aunt Rosy looked at me with a question-mark look on her face, and said to me. "Well wasn't the pie difficult to eat? I didn't have time to bake, today, so I had just taken it out of the freezer and it was frozen solid."

FOUR TALES OF OUR DOG, LADY

Our Convent, a four-bedroom house, was located right at the very end of town. In fact, the woods were right across the road in front of the Convent—actually, the Convent was, so to speak, in the woods. There was a lovely creek right across from the Convent, as well; and at night, with your bedroom window opened, you could hear the gurgling water of the creek as it flowed down over the rocks, lulling our bodies to a peaceful sleep.

Tale # 1: We Must Not Let the Pastor Know About Our Dog, Lady

Our Convent had a large glassed-in porch; and since it was at the end of town, oft times transients would pick our porch to sleep in at night, as we had a wicker couch that they could sleep on. We had not intended for it to be used for this purpose; and so our Superior, being very nervous about this situation, decided that we needed to have a dog to protect us.

One afternoon, she arrived with an adorable Alaskan Husky puppy, and we all fell in love with her at first sight. Well, I shouldn't have said "we all"—one of our sisters, Sister Alicia, was not a bit happy. She did not like dogs. She also did not like the fact that they had hair, and she just knew that there would be hair all over the Convent. Sister Superior suggested that we let Sister Marta, an elderly nun, name the dog. She also told Sister Marta that she would be responsible for taking care of her, as well. Sister Marta was delighted to no end, as she loved dogs; and with a big smile on her face, she said, "Her name will be Lady." And so it was.

Lady's color was gray and white, and she had a tail that curled right into a circle. If she was unhappy, the tail would go straight down. It was decided that we would not mention her to the Pastor, Father Anselm, as we knew that he would not approve one bit of us having a dog in the Convent. Father, by his demeanor, made everyone aware of his social position. Not only was he a priest, but also he had a Doctoral degree in Divinity. He liked to refer to himself as "The Father." A lot of the time, you would see him wearing his Doctoral Robe. He was a slim, tall man who was very proper and serious, and who did not take well to what he would consider foolish or a waste of time.

Father also really did not approve of me and my behavior. How do I know this to be true? Well, one day after Sunday Mass, he called me over by gesturing with one hand (the other hand was hidden by his Doctoral robe). Picking up on his signal, I went over to him. He was taller than me, and with a solemn face he looked at me and said, "Sister, I understand you are going on retreat for a week." I answered yes. Still with a very serious face, he said to me, "Sister, I want you to pray for a very special intention. Will you promise me you will pray very hard?" I nodded yes, and he went on and said, "Now, you promise me you will pray for this special intention." Again I nodded yes. Then he said to me, "I want you to pray to God that you will not be so frivolous." With that, he turned around and walked away. I'm afraid that prayer was never answered.

You most likely are confused right now, as this tale is about our dog Lady, yet I've been talking about our Pastor and me. However, there is a method to my madness; for both will be part of this tale.

This one day, Father came over to the Convent wearing his Doctoral robe. Mind you, he hardly ever came to the Convent, so when he did we knew it was something of an important matter—either something that he wanted us to do, or matters pertaining to the Parish itself, or even at times letting us know of his displeasure if we did not meet the standards that he had set for us. Sister Marta opened the door, and Father came in and sat down in a high, straight-back chair covered in cloth with a pleated skirt that reached from the seat of the chair to the floor. Sister Marta summoned all of us to the living room, and we came in and acknowledged Father with a "Hello," then all sat down. Father started talking to us about his concerns—when all of a sudden he jumped up from his chair, yelling, " I've been bit, I've been bit!" At the same time he was yelling, he was also dancing around the floor, pain showing on his face.

At first we didn't know what was going on, and we jumped from our chairs and stood there in a comatose position as we watched him, wondering what was happening to him. It was so out of character for him to be behaving this way. Just then, our puppy Lady came running out from under his chair, wagging her tale. At that moment, we realized what had happened. Being a puppy, Lady had sharp, needle-like teeth, and she had bitten Father in his Achilles heel. After the first shock of pain, he turned and gave us a look of disdain. And, limping as he crossed the floor, he promptly left. I have often wondered what hurt him the most: the bite on his heel, or the fact that he had lost his dignity in front of us.

Tale # 2: Lady and Sister Alicia

We worked not only in our own Parish, but in two other parishes, as well. In one of them, we became really close friends with the Pastor, Father O'Flynn. We would work for him in his Parish every Friday for the full day. He and his housekeeper, Mary, would provide lunch for us. I loved it, as Mary was a great cook.

One of Father O'Flynn's endearing charms was his sense of humor. He was always ready for a good laugh. He also loved to tease—and if his teasing could cause a little embarrassment, all the better. Mind you, now, he was very kind-hearted and would never cause any pain or hurt by his teasing. He also was a very warm and loquacious man.

Every Sunday evening, Father O'Flynn would come over for tea and pastries, along with having a good chat with all of us. As said, he loved to tease but never where it would cause any hurt—but maybe a little annoyance, or making the person a little peeved or embarrassed. Did he get a kick out of it? Yeah, just a wee bit. Father especially loved to tease Sister Alicia, who was always very vulnerable in that regard; and in all honesty, Sister was lacking when it came to a sense of humor—which, for Father, would make teasing her even better. All in all, however, she still really liked him very much.

As I have mentioned, we did not eat with others, so if anyone came to the front door, the first Sister who was finished or close to being finished with her meal would be the one to go answer it. This Saturday, it happened to be Sister Alicia who had finished her meal first, so she went and opened the door, and invited Father O'Flynn into the living room. Father had his favorite large armchair that he sat in every time he came; and when he would sit down, his large belly took over his whole lap. I often thought that Clement Clarke Moore, who wrote "The Night Before Christmas," must have known some one like Father, as Father's belly really did "shake like a bowl full of jelly" when he laughed. Around Christmas time, I would look at him and think to myself, *My, he would make a wonderful Santa Claus. All he would need was a white beard and Santa's clothes. are the clothes.*

After Father was seated, Sister Alicia was still standing up, facing him. And knowing that we had our puppy, Lady, he asked her, "Sister, is your puppy housebroken?"

In a sharp, dignified voice, Sister Alicia replied, "Why of course she is!"

Then he asked her a second time, "Are you sure, now, that she is housebroken?"

This time, with even more irritation in her voice, Sister said, "Yes, of course she is!"

Father O'Flynn then said to her, "Sister, if that is so, then please tell me why you have a puddle of pee under your feet."

Sister Alicia looked down—and there she was, standing right in the middle where Lady had peed on the floor. Saying that Sister's dignity was bruised would be the understatement of the year, since she was so prim and proper. And with a red face, she stomped out of the room, with Father breaking out in peals of laughter.

Tale # 3: Lady, Don't You Know You've Got It All Wrong??

Sister Superior was delighted that our dog, Lady, grew into a wonderful watchdog. However, she soon found out that our watchdog was very selective when it came to men. If questionable men would come to the door or walk past our house into the woods, our dog, Lady, would run over to them wagging her tail, jumping all over them, and begging to get petted. She even was very generous with her kisses, lapping away at their faces as they would bend over to pet her.

However, when other men, like our Pastor or visiting Priest, would come to the Convent, Lady would growl and show her teeth and try to get at them. We would have to hurry and intervene so she wouldn't bite them. When we knew they would be coming, we always made sure that Lady was locked in the other room. After the incident with our pastor, when Lady bit him in the foot, we were very faithful about making sure she was locked up.

It was in the fall when, unexpectedly, the Vicar General of the Catholic Diocese, who was ranked in Clerical order next to the Catholic Bishop, came to visit us at the Convent. Sister Superior just happened to be the one who saw him walking up the sidewalk. She hurried and called all of us into the living room, and then went to the door. Meanwhile, none of us happened to notice that Lady was lying down next to the sofa when

Sister Superior opened the door for him to come in. Up jumped our dog, Lady, from the floor—and before any of us could get her, she ran right over to the Vicar. Our hearts were in our throats, as she was so fast that not even Sister Superior could restrain her. We all just *knew* that Lady was going to try and bite him, like she did with the other priests. And biting the Vicar General was the very worst of all.

However, to our amazement and surprise, Lady, wagging her tale, started jumping all over him to be petted. Sister Superior was so embarrassed and flustered by Lady's behavior of jumping up and putting her paws on his nice black pants that she went to apologize to the Vicar. She said to him, "Who would have ever guessed that our dog would like you so much? When it comes to decent, respectable men of worth, Lady always becomes very vicious and mean and tries to bite them. Yet when it comes to bums and undesirables, she really loves them and jumps all over them to get petted, just like she did with you!"

Tale # 4: A Mutual Arrangement

I really loved our dog, Lady, and I knew she loved me, as well – especially when it came to mealtime. Lady was very smart, and when it came time for us to eat, she would get under the table and put her head on my lap.

Here, I need to mention that the Superior's Orders were that we had to eat the food that was placed before us, whether we liked it our not. I especially did not like liver at all. Even as a child, I would not eat it. But as Sister Superior loved liver, we had it very often.

So what I would do was to *pretend* that I was eating it; and then, when I knew that the Superior wasn't looking, I would slip my piece of liver to Lady under the table. She was one happy dog, and I was one happy woman.

Tale # 5: Another Dog Tale

This tale is not about our dog, Lady. However, since I am on the subject of dogs, I decided to include this tale as well.

In one Parish where I worked, our Pastor had two poodle dogs, one female and one male. When the female dog became pregnant, he brought her over to the Convent for us to look after her until she gave birth to her puppies. She became my responsibility; and never having been around a dog giving birth before, I was quite uncertain as to what I was supposed to do. However, bless the mother dog, *she* knew what to do, and she had just one baby without my being around. I fell in love with the puppy—it was love at first sight—and so I asked the Pastor if I could keep her. With great relief, he said yes, he would be most happy for us to have her.

There were only two of us there in the Convent. I had just been made the Superior, no big thing. I told the other Sister as far as I was concerned, there *was* no Superior: we both were equals, and I would just do the work that was required of me as a Superior.

Some months passed by, and Christmas time came. It was always a very busy time for both of us—not only with the Church choir and the children's Nativity pageant and concert, but also because we would visit the Hospital, and the Retirement and Nursing homes for the elderly. We would bring a group of our children to sing some carols, and then we would pass out the gifts we had for them. We would also go to visit seniors who were shut-ins in their homes, first checking to make sure that our visit would be appreciated before we went.

This Christmas, we decided to buy large net Christmas stockings and fill them with small gifts, cookies, and candy, etc. Then we would place them in large cartons to carry them to the places where we were going.

The night before our venture to the Nursing Homes, we had our Christmas pageant with our grade-school children over in the Church. Just as we were getting ready to leave, our Pastor came to the door and told us that he would like his two dogs to stay here in the Convent, as he was going to have company stop in at the Rectory after the Christmas pageant. So we said we would be glad to do it. We knew that our puppy would like the company, as well.

The other Sister had already gone over to the Church for the pageant; I just had to finish stuffing the last Christmas stocking before I left to join her. When that was done, I put it in the box, and then stood there looking at the results of all my hard work. I smiled with pride as I looked at the other boxes filled with all the stockings, lined up in the kitchen by the back door. I could just see the smiling faces of the recipients as they received their gift.

That evening, after the pageant was over, Sister and I headed back to the Convent. As I opened the door, what to my wondering eyes did appear? No, it wasn't Santa Clause or his reindeer; it was all the stockings all torn open and scattered all over the kitchen floor, and the gifts, cookies, candy, and nuts strewn all over the place. It was very evident who the culprits were. I had a hard time with my emotions: I didn't know whether to laugh or cry. We had to admit that it was funny, and yet it was tragic as well—all my work gone for naught.

And no wonder the dogs were sleeping when we came in. For the cookies and candy were not only in the kitchen, but in the living room and bedrooms, as well. The beds were all messed up where the dogs had buried their treasures of cookies and candy. Later on, Sister and I even found cookies under the couch and chair pillows, where the dogs had buried them, as well.

The dogs waking up came running to us with their tails wagging. What could we do except acknowledge and pet them? After all, I was their Santa Claus, and I was the one who had left all those wonderful gifts. At our expense, those dogs had the happiest Christmas ever.

HALLOWEEN AND CHRISTMAS IN UPPER NEW YORK STATE

Tale # 1: The First Halloween Party

The Parish where I was sent never had Catholic Sisters there before we came. We were sent there at the invitation of the Bishop to not only work in our Parish but also in three other Parishes as well. They all would benefit by having us there, working in the community as well as in the churches. Our work was not only Catechetical but also what you would call Social Service Work. There were four of us Sisters working there, all living in one Convent. The week was divided up so that we Sisters could work in all four Parishes.

Shortly after we arrived, we soon found out that we were not appreciated by two women. Actually, you might say that these women, more than the Pastor, ran the Parish, as they seemed to be in control of everything. These two women resented us for being there and taking over all that they had been in charge of for many, many, years. In a way, I can see their side of it and understand how they felt about losing control and their status of being in charge of everything.

Right away, we found out that taking over was not going to be as easy as we had hoped: the two women were (excuse the expression) like "bad weeds": they just kept showing up like the KGB when we were using the Church, or in the kitchen in back of the hall. They still considered the Church and hall to be *their* territory, and they were going to protect and defend it.

Halloween had approached, and we were having the Halloween party in the Church hall for all the children in the Parish, knowing that the two women had already given us a list of do's and don'ts about using the Church, the hall, and the kitchen. The Superior had us wait until late at night (when she felt the two women would most likely be at home and asleep in their beds) to go over to the Church and decorate for the Halloween party.

We decorated, set up the tables, and had the hall looking very festive. As our Superior was Italian and had worked as a nun in the orphanage in Rome, Italy, she decided that we should have spaghetti for the children, and designated me to make the spaghetti. It was my first time making spaghetti for that many children, so I was not too happy about my assignment. Early the next morning, I went down to the kitchen with all the ingredients for the spaghetti, took out the large pots from the cupboard that we were told we were not to use, and prayed that the women would not come in and catch me using them until I had my spaghetti made. Thanks to the dear Lord, they did not show up until later that afternoon.

The children had all arrived for the party featuring games, eating, and having fun being together. The party was well underway and really going strong when here came the two women into the hall. Oh, how I wish you could have seen their faces—were they ever upset! Their clean kitchen and tidy hall

all looked like a disaster area, with crumbs on the floor from the cupcakes, cookies, etc.; and in the kitchen, there was spaghetti sauce on the stove, counter, and floor from dishing out the spaghetti onto paper plates. On top of it all, there were the kids running around, playing and eating and having a great time. The two women also started running around, telling the children, "Don't spill your drink," "Watch, don't drop food on the floor," "Get down from sitting on the counter," and so on.

When the two women saw kids up on the stage, they ran up to chase them off, waving their arms and yelling, "Get off our stage! You are not to be up here! Now get off!" The reason why the women did not want them on the stage was that they had it set up like a living room— with two wicker chairs; a couch; two end tables on either side of the couch holding two huge lamps, with green horse-heads as the lamp base; and a large carpet on the stage floor.

Then one of the women came into the kitchen and yelled at me: "Look at this kitchen! You just look at it, there's spaghetti sauce all over! And who told you that you could use the kitchen?"

I replied, "The Superior."

She just looked at me and scowled, and both women left the hall in anger.

Of course, after the party was over, we four sisters cleaned up the hall and kitchen and left with everything just as clean and tidy as we had found it.

The next day, there was a letter inside the screen door on our front porch. It contained a whole list of all the do's and don'ts of using the hall, and said that they were going to report us to the Pastor for lack of respect for them and for the hall. We just looked at each other, shaking our heads. Sister Superior took the letter and, with strong deliberation, tore it into pieces and threw it in the wastepaper basket. The two ladies may have been very unhappy; however, the children at the party were very, very happy and looking forward to the next Halloween.

Tale # 2: The Second Year—Another Halloween

It was time again to have our Halloween Party in the Church hall. Ignoring the angry notes from the two ladies, late on the eve of the party, all four of us Sisters went down to the Church hall like we had the last time. We divided up the jobs of decorating and setting up the tables, etc., with the intention that whoever finished first would help out wherever help was needed.

I asked if I could make the stage into a cemetery, and was given the green light, so to speak. I had made up large tombstones out of heavy white cardboard paper at home, and now I propped them up in the back so that they would stand up, just like stones in a cemetery. I also drew pictures on the cardboard stones, along with epitaphs, to make them look as realistic as possible. The pleasure of doing it also came from the imp inside me, knowing how distraught the two ladies would be when they saw the stage.

Before I go on any further, I need to tell you that I did not fit the norm or decorum expected from a Catholic Sister. (You most likely already know this by my other tales.) I was in my early twenties, at this time. In making the tomb-stones for the stage, instead of saying "Satan, get behind me," I gave in to my temptations and—as Eliza Doolittle would say in "My Fair Lady"—"I'm goin' to get a little of my own back." On one stone, I drew a foot; and in the heel of the foot was a jagged, gaping hole made to look like a dog's bite, with blood dripping down from the wound. The epitaph read: "Here lies the remains of poor Tom Toot! It's sad to say he died from being bitten in the Foot." If you remember the tale of Father O'Flynn and our dog, Lady, biting him in the heel of his foot, you won't need to think twice as to whom this tombstone referred to and the incident that took place.

Then the other tombstone was for the one of the two ladies who gave us such a very hard time. I drew a picture of a lady's head with her hair in a topknot; and around her throat was a rope, with the other part of the rope going up over her head. The epitaph read: "Here lies the remains of an old schoolmarm. We found her body hanging in the barn." I know that both she and Father saw these "tombstones," as they were there to make sure that order would be kept during the party.

To my surprise, neither of them ever said a word about it. I'm sure they knew, and I'm also sure they knew that it was I—the one they considered the "frivolous Sister"—who was responsible for the artwork and epitaph! Yes, you don't have to tell me for certain I was not a regular nun!

Tale # 3: That Same Year on Halloween Night

The afternoon Halloween party was over with, and we left the hall clean and tidy as we did the last time, also knowing that this year too, the next day a letter would be sent to us. We came home, and after the evening meal and prayers, we just relaxed and took it easy in our living room.

One of the younger women in the Parish came over to the Convent to see me. Like me, there was an impish side to her, as well. Since it was Halloween night, she came to the Convent all decked out in a costume; and in her arms was a large horse blanket and a scary mask. "Here, Sister," she said to me. "Put this on, and let's go Trick-or-Treating over at Father O'Flynn's house." I thought to myself, *Oh, how fun!* Then I turned and looked at Sister Superior. She, too, must have liked the idea, because she nodded that yes, I could go with the young woman.

With Sister Superior's permission, I took the mask, put it over my headgear and face, and then also covered myself with the large blanket. It was perfect for a disguise: I knew there was no way Father would recognize me. So off we went to Father O'Flynn's house. What we hadn't planned on was the Rectory's front-porch light being turned off, and the front windows also being in darkness. My friend turned to me and said, "Okay, Sister, let's go to the back door. I see the porch light is on, and there is a light in the kitchen." We went to the back door, opened the enclosed porch door, and rang the doorbell.

But instead of Father coming to the door, as we had hoped he would, it was his elderly housekeeper. Just as my friend was saying "Trick or Treat," the housekeeper—noticing that we were adults—look at us with fear in her face started screaming, "Father, come here quick! Father, come here! These are not children, they are adults." Seeing that we had upset her so badly, and also knowing that the Priest would not let us go until he found out our identity, my friend and I turned to run away. But as we did so, the housekeeper grabbed hold of me around my waist. Being stronger than her, I was able to get away from her embrace, and I ran from the porch to join my friend, who also was running to the car for our getaway.

When we got into the car, I said to my friend, "I'm sure she knows who I am." My friend tried to reassure me that in no way whatsoever could the housekeeper know, as I was so well covered by the blanket and mask. I felt reassured for a while; but later on that evening, I got to thinking, *Surely, she could feel the rosary beads that hung down from the thick cord.* Still, I tried to convince myself that it was impossible for the housekeeper to feel anything, as the blanket was so heavy and thick.

Time went by, and the Pastor never said a word about that night, nor did he act any differently toward me. So I felt relieved that I had gotten away with my misadventure—until one weekend, when The Father, (as he called himself, wearing his Doctoral robe), Sister Superior, and yours truly were riding back in his car from services at our other mission Church. Father drove for a while without saying a word. He had his rear-view mirror positioned so that he could see me sitting in the back seat; and as he started looking at me in the rear-view mirror, he said to Sister Superior, "Sister, did you get the music signboard finished yet, like you promised, so we can get it put up in the Church?"

Sister Superior proceeded to tell him that we were way too busy, and that each of us Sisters was so loaded with work that none of us had had a chance to get the signboard finished as of yet. The Pastor, still looking at me through the mirror, said to her, "Well, if the Sister in the back seat of this car had put all her energy and time into working on the signboard rather than dressing up on Halloween, the signboard would have been done, now."

CHRISTMAS IN THE SAME TOWN

Tale # 1: The Lamb That Stole the Show

Many people have put on Christmas plays, but I wonder if any has been as unique as the one we put on the week before Christmas. The title of the play was "The Little Lame Lamb." Almost all the scenes in the play took place on a hillside. Sister Superior, wanting the play to be as realistic as possible, decided to imitate the way plays were done in Italy: using live animals in their productions. So this Christmas, she decided to have a real live lamb in the play.

I did not know this when I came home in the late afternoon from teaching my class. I had just entered the kitchen when Sister Superior turned around from where she was stirring the pot on the stove and said to me, "Sister, I am putting you in charge of caring for the little lamb that's in the old shed. We will be using him in the Christmas play." Sister had gotten the live lamb from a woman whom we called "Pearl of Great Price," since her name was Pearl.

I said, "A lamb, a real live lamb in the play?"

She looked a little irritated that I would question her use of a real lamb in the play, and she responded again, more emphatically this time, "Yes, a real live lamb." Then she said, "I want you to go out there before you take your cloak off "—the cloak took the place of a warm coat—"and feed the lamb. He must be hungry by now."

I said, "But Sister, what about Father Paul? He won't like it; and the two old ladies who think they own the hall—boy, are they going to be angry and upset when they see a live lamb on their precious stage."

Sister Superior proceeded to tell me that there was nothing wrong with having a live lamb onstage, as they always used them in Italy; and besides, that was none of my worry. And she told me again to go and feed the lamb. So I left and headed for the old shed. And as I was walking, I thought to myself, *I never have lived on a farm, and I don't know the first thing about caring for the lamb. I may have taken the vow of obedience—but being asked to do this task is ridiculous.*

Mind you, I am an animal lover; but how in the world was I going to take care of this lamb? I opened the door and went into the shed—and I was shocked! Instead of being a lamb, it was a huge male sheep. It had dark yellow-brownish wool hanging down underneath its belly from lying down in animal poop and urine. And did it ever smell.

I thought to myself, *If I'm going to take care of this sheep, I'm going to have to get rid of this smell. It is making me sick!* So I went back to the Convent to get a pair of scissors to cut the dirty hair hanging down from the sheep's belly so it would smell better. I got the scissors; and as I was leaving, I said to Sister Marta, who was sitting at the kitchen table correcting papers, "That's not a lamb, out there. It's a stinky-filthy sheep! A dirty, stinking sheep!"

Then I left and went back into the shed; and I started to cut the wool with the scissors. But to my dismay, the scissors could not cut through the wool; it was like trying to cut through heavy rubber. I tried and tried, but I just couldn't cut it. I was so upset by this, as I did not want to care for the sheep with this horrible smell. I just knew I had to do something. Just then, a light went on in my brain, so to speak. I went back to the Convent and took the large can of Johnson's Baby Powder (the only kind of powder we were allowed to use), and I doused the baby powder all over the sheep to try and camouflage the smell.

On the day of the performance, I tried to talk Sister Superior out of using the sheep in the play, but to no avail. Once Sister made up her mind, nothing could change it!

The next problem was getting the sheep down to the Church, which was four blocks away. So I asked Sister Superior how was I going to manage that problem? She promptly told me not to worry; that Pearl had told her that the way to get the sheep down to the Church was to feed it pieces of bread, as it would go after the bread. All I needed to do was to drop the pieces of bread as I walked the sheep down to the Church. She also wanted me to stay behind at the Convent until twenty minutes before the play was to start. Then I was to bring the sheep down to the Church hall, as she didn't want anyone to see it until the play started. The Church hall was in the basement of the Church, and had two entrances—one in front and one in back where the stage was located. That way, the sheep could be taken downstairs and put on the stage without anyone seeing him until the curtain opened.

The two women had somehow found out the time of the rehearsals for the play, and would come and sit in front of the stage to make certain that we would not touch any of their furniture or remove it from the stage. As I mentioned before, they had the stage set like a living room, with a rug on the floor, a wicker couch, two chairs, and two end tables with green horsehead lamps on them.

So the night before the play, just as we had for Halloween, we went down to the Church late at night, with all the scenery sets that had been made at the Convent. And again like the last time, we did this so that the two women would not see them until the next day, by which time it would be too late for them to do anything about it. Actually, the furniture really came in handy; we used it to hold up our scenery of bushes and landscape, so for us the furniture made perfect props for our scenery—and how would the ladies know, as the props would be hiding it all?

Newspaper was spread all over the floor, so that if the sheep pooped it would not damage the carpet. We also took a roll of linoleum that was to be put down in the kitchen. Seeing that it was just the perfect size for the large log that we needed, we wrapped it in brown butcher paper, then painted a couple of knot-holes on it, and it really did look like a log. The log was placed right in front of the stage. With the log covered, how would the ladies know it was their linoleum that we were to leave alone and not to touch at all?

The time came for me to bring the sheep down to the Church. I went to the shed, carrying a bag with pieces of bread inside it. I took a piece of bread out and, sure enough, it worked: the sheep started to follow me. So I kept doing the same thing, feeling really good at how easy it was to take the sheep down to the Church.

But what I hadn't anticipated were the neighbors' dogs. Halfway down the block, out came one dog, and then another dog, barking and running after the sheep. The sheep turned around and started running for the Convent—and there I was, trying to chase the dogs to go back home. Then I started running down the block after the sheep, and finally I caught up to it. To say I was stressed out by all this would be an understatement, for sure. And another problem: how in the world would I get that sheep down to the Church? It was almost time for the play to start, and if I didn't have that sheep there, I would be in big trouble with my Superior. And that would not have been a good thing – believe me!

Then I came up with the idea of taking the sheep down to the Church in our station wagon, as there was ample cargo space inside at the back of the wagon, with a door that would open to make a platform for sliding heavy stuff into the station wagon. But there was another problem: the wagon was high up from the ground. How in heaven's name was I going to get the sheep up into it? The sheep was way too heavy for me to lift him, yet I knew I had to get him into the station wagon. It must have been with the help of the Holy Spirit, for I came up with the idea of getting one of the wooden planks we had on the side of the shed, and using it for a ramp leading from the road up into the back of the wagon.

I had to hurry, as time was flying by so fast. So I ran and got the plank and put it in place, and then went over to the sheep—which was just standing there, chewing the grass on our lawn. Using the bread, I coaxed the sheep up into the back of the wagon, and off we went. Just imagine what a scene that made! Here was a nun in a full habit, driving with a huge sheep standing up in the back of the station wagon.

I finally reached the church and was most grateful that I had time to spare—I wasn't late. Getting the sheep onstage was no trouble at all. We had hay strewn over the newspaper on the floor for the sheep to eat—and also, we were hoping, to keep it in one place. The hay was placed right behind the log, where the sheep would be, and I would be standing offstage behind the curtain, next to the log, with the bread close by in case we needed it.

No one in the audience could see me. However, I could see them; and when the curtain opened up on the first act, I saw our Pastor and the two women sitting right in the front row. When they saw the sheep onstage—well, I wish you could have seen the expression on their faces. It spoke louder than words.

To say that they were upset by the sight of the sheep onstage, along with the straw, etc., would be the understatement of the year. In fact, Father got up from his chair and walked right out. We didn't need to ask him what he thought about the sheep; it was very evident by his absence. The sheep looked very intelligent as he chewed away on the hay, and did not seem a bit disturbed by the children's presence onstage. I peeked out from the side curtain and looked out at the audience. It was noticeable that the sheep became the main star of the show.

The first act of the play went along smoothly. However, toward the end of the second act, it was completely a different story. The sheep started getting restless, and was no longer interested in eating his hay. Seeing his restlessness, I started throwing pieces of bread onto the stage. However the scenery onstage looked more enticing to him. The next thing we knew, the sheep was tearing the paper off the log, exposing the linoleum; and then he proceeded to go over and start chewing on the scenery. The children were still saying their lines, but what they said could not be heard over the laughter that was coming from the audience. And the sheep, not being bothered by either, kept tearing down the scenery—and along with it, exposing the most treasured horse-head lamps and the wicker chairs, which were in full view to the two old ladies. Not only that, but by now the scenery was in shreds and the audience in peals of laughter.

The two women got up in disgust and left. Of course, the play ended during the second act. Need you ask why??

Tale # 2: What Is This?

It was a week after Christmas. (In the Catholic Church, Christmas starts on Christmas Eve and lasts for fourteen days. However, we would start our religion classes the same time that public school would begin after Christmas Holidays.) I was teaching the third grade and still feeling the let-down from all the pre-Christmas activities and celebrating the Christmas week, itself. I did not feel like teaching that day; but since there was no one else to take my place I had no choice but to teach the class.

Looking for an easy way out of teaching, I decided to read the story of the "Flight into Egypt" from the Bible. At that time, we did not have the new translation of the Bible, and the old version had a lot of "Thee's, Thy's, and Thou's." I read to the children the Christmas story of Mary and Joseph with the Baby Jesus going into Egypt to escape from King Herod.

After I had finished reading the story, I decided to have the children draw a picture about the story they had just heard, and then color their picture. I passed out the paper, pencils and crayons to the children so that they could draw and color their pictures. Then I sat down behind my desk, just relaxing and letting the children do the work.

One little girl was finished with her picture, and she came up to me so I could look at her masterpiece and give her my approval. As I was looking at her picture, I said to her: "Here is Joseph, and here is Mary on the donkey holding Baby

Jesus in her arms." I wanted the girl to be happy that I could recognize everyone in her picture.

As I was still looking at the picture, I saw a strange little dot with four small lines coming out from it; and I knew that it held some significance to the child, but I didn't have a clue as to what it could be. So I asked her, "What is this little dot, here?"

She looked at me very seriously and replied, as if I should have known, "It's a flea."

I looked at her and said, "A flea?"

She nodded yes, took the picture, and went back to her seat.

I asked myself a couple of times, *A flea. Why would she draw a flea?* And then it suddenly dawned on me: in the Bible story that I read to the children, the Angel said to Joseph, "Take thy mother and child and flee into Egypt."

WINTER TIME IN UPPER NEW YORK STATE

The Convent where I was stationed was in Upper New York State. Our Convent was located right in the woods, and it really was a lovely area for us to live in, as it was full of rolling hills with lots of green growth and trees. Right across the dirt road in front of the Convent was the other part of the woods; and in the backyard of the Convent there was a lovely sloping hill, which went all the way down to a little flat area. Across from it was another hill. In the wintertime, we always had a lot of snow. This made the hill just perfect for skiing or sledding, as there was something like a pathway between the trees that went all the way down the hill to the very bottom.

When I was in my twenties in Upper New York State, I was full of vim and vigor, and always willing to try and do something new. The other three Sisters, who all were quite a bit older than me, did not really feel that I was behaving the way a nun should be; they felt I lacked religious decorum. Nevertheless, they did not keep me from my adventures.

There was a middle-aged widow named Beth who lived alone, not too far down the street from us. We would take turns visiting with her so she would not feel too lonely. This one winter day, I was visiting with her and she asked me if I knew how to ski. I answered, "No, my mother would not let me ski when I was growing up." My mother was always over-protective of me. Mind you, she would have died of a stroke if she could have seen some of the things I did when I was away from her – like climbing up on the roofs of barns, climbing up the side of a silo to the top—going over the waterfalls in an irrigation ditch to learn how to swim—climbing up trees, pretending it was my plane—or leaping from one branch to another, pretending I was a monkey. I could go on and on with my adventures (or should I say misadventures?). However, I will stop here, as I know you have a good idea of what I was like growing up.

Now that I have sidetracked you, I will go back to my story.

After I told Beth that I never did ski, she asked me if I would like to try, as she had a pair of skis and would be most happy to give them to me. Giving her a big smile, I said, "Oh yes, I would love to have your skis." So she gave them to me; and I left her home, walking back to the Convent one happy nun, carrying my pair of skis.

We had an hour's recreation time in the afternoons and after supper in the evenings; and on Sundays after Church, we had the day to ourselves. The next day was Sunday and I could hardly wait to try out my skis. Beth had showed me how to put them on my feet. They were the kind where you just slid your foot in them; and when you would fall, most times the skis would come right off your feet.

Here I was, at the top of the hill, standing all alone with my skis on and a ski pole in both hands—not knowing that on a steep hill, you usually slalom down the hill. I went straight down, and it was so exhilarating feeling the icy wind blowing against my face as I was speeding on. I started getting close to the bottom, when the thought struck me like a thunderbolt: *How do I stop when I get to the bottom?* Thank God, there was enough virgin snow to provide a very soft cushion as I proceeded to fall down in a sitting position when I reached the bottom. I found that it worked just fine. What I didn't enjoy was trudging up the hill, but the fun of going down really made up for it.

A SIN TO SHOW YOUR HAIR

Forty years ago it was forbidden for anyone to see your hair. We did not have our heads shaved, unless the Sister wanted it. Most of us just kept our hair very short. (This all ended in the late 1960s.) Even we Sisters were not allowed to see each other's hair. In fact, at bedtime we would wear a cap on our head so that when we went to the bathroom to do our nightly ablutions, our head would be covered. We even wore our nightcap to bed every night. We also were not allowed to see each other unclothed, which may seem strange to some nowadays.

Why am I telling you this? So that you will understand the humor in the following stories.

Tale # 1: The Headless Nun

One Sunday afternoon, three girls and two boys from the local junior high school came over to the Convent carrying with them a toboggan, and asked for me to come out and go tobogganing with them. I did so for a while. Then I decided to ask the other Sisters to come and join us.

After much pleading on my side for one of the Sisters to go down the hill with me, she got on behind me on the toboggan. As we were going down the hill, all of a sudden I heard her cry out, "I lost my head! I lost my head!" I thought to myself, *She couldn't have lost her head, or she wouldn't be yelling like she is.* And I couldn't stop the toboggan until we reached the bottom, it was going so fast down the hill.

When we reached the bottom of the hill, I got up and turned and looked—and truly, I couldn't see Sister's head at all. She looked like the headless horseman! We wore large cloaks rather than coats, and she had put the cloak up over her head. I asked her, "Are you all right?" and the voice underneath the cloak said, "No, I lost my head." As she said that, I could hear the kids at the top of the hill laughing away. And as I looked up, I saw Sister's headgear—which had covered all of her head except for the face— all in one piece hanging down from a branch just up the hill a-ways.

You may wonder why she had her head covered. Well, at that period of time in the Convent life, it was strictly forbidden for anyone to see your hair, as hair was considered the crowning glory of every woman. It was considered almost as bad as being naked (though not quite as much). So here was Sister, sitting on the toboggan, with her head completely covered over by her cloak, still yelling, "I lost my head!"

I trudged up the hill, grabbed hold of her headgear that had come off all in one piece, brought it down to where Sister was still sitting with all of her head covered, and handed it to her through the opening of her cloak. Then I took hold of the cloak and pulled it up, using it like a tent over her, until she got her headgear back on. The kids were still laughing as she got up from the toboggan and trudged back up the hill. She didn't look at them as she passed them to make her flight into the Convent.

Needless to say, she was not a bit happy with her toboggan ride, nor with my having coaxed her to come on the toboggan. And she showed her displeasure by giving me one of those looks each time we were together, that evening. End of this tale! Amen!

Tale # 2: A Quick Cover

As soap is to the body, so laughter is to the soul.

— Jewish Proverb

During the Holidays, we three Sisters and four of our other Sisters whose Convent was a couple of hours away would alternate going to each other's Convent to spend the Holiday time together. It so happened that this Holiday, it was our turn to go to the other Sisters' Convent the day after Christmas. One of our Sisters had just come to live with us that September, and had never been at the other Convent before, so this would be a new experience for her.

We left late on a Friday afternoon and arrived at our Sisters' place just before suppertime. After eating, we all gathered together in the community room for an evening of good conversation and fun. This Convent was a large home, and all the bedrooms were up on the second floor. The bathroom was unique for those of us visiting, as it had two doors by which you could enter the bathroom—from either the hallway or one of the bedrooms.

The new Sister decided that she needed to go to bed, and she also wanted to take a bath before she retired for the night. So off she went and filled up the tub with nice warm water, and made certain that the door leading into the bathroom from the hallway was locked. However, she forgot to check the other door to make certain that it was locked, as well. She then climbed down into the tub and was taking a nice relaxing bath, when all of a sudden the unlocked door opened—and in walked a Sister from the bedroom, oblivious to the fact of the Sister bathing in the tub.

The shocked Sister in the tub, seeing her come in, was so caught off-guard that she became very flustered. She did not know what to do—and realizing that her head was uncovered (in that moment, she never gave a thought to the fact that she was stark naked, which was even worse), instead of grabbing a towel to cover herself, she hurriedly took the washcloth and immediately placed it on the top of her head to cover her hair. And so there she was, in all her naked glory, sitting in the tub with a washcloth on her head.

Yes! This definitely is a true tale. Again, I will say: AMEN!

STATIONED IN EASTERN OREGON

"You Crashed My Gate!"

In the late 1960s, I was stationed in a small town in Oregon. I happened to be the only Sister who could drive a car, so any time a Sister needed to go somewhere further than she could walk, I would be the one to drive her to her destination.

On one occasion, an Aunt of one of the Sisters came from New York and stayed with us for a week. Not having an airport in our town, we would have to drive over a mountain pass to the following small city. The mountain road was very narrow—it only had two lanes—and it also was very curvy, which curtailed driving very fast and made the trip take longer.

We really enjoyed the Sister's Aunt, and it was nice having her visiting us. The day arrived when it was time for her to leave and go back to New York; so that morning, the Sister and her Aunt got into the car, I got behind the wheel, and we were off to the airport.

As Murphy's Law would have it, we ran into road construction on the mountain pass, which caused a big delay in our getting to the airport. Was I ever happy to see the town with the airport in view, as I knew we had no time to spare whatsoever. Driving faster, I got on the road that led to the airport.

Now I must mention something else: not only was the airport there but right next to it was the Air Force Base as well. The road I was traveling on was the same for both the airport and the Air Force Base, and the road divided right before you entered either one.

As I was driving down this road, I could see the landing strip with the plane that the Aunt was to leave on—it had already arrived—and I knew it would not be too long before it took off. I was so worried about the plane taking off before we got there that I was fixated on looking at the plane instead of where I was going.

At that moment, I heard a sound like someone screaming, so I looked through the rear- view mirror to see what the yelling was all about, when I saw this young Air Force man running right behind me, waving his gun for me to stop. It was far beyond me why he was chasing my car and yelling like a crazy man. And as he came closer, we could hear him yelling, "You crashed my gate! You crashed my gate!" I thought to myself, *I don't remember crashing any gate – how could I have done that without knowing it?*

Seeing that he was still chasing me, I stopped the car and rolled the window down on my side. He came over to me, and he was really in a terrible state as he yelled at me again at the top of his voice, "You Crashed My Gate!" But the next words out of his mouth really alarmed me, and fear set in as he shouted, "I'm suppose to shoot you! You Crashed My Gate! You're lucky to be alive—I am supposed to shoot you!"

I looked at him in astonishment and said, "Why do you want to shoot us?"

"You Crashed My Gate! You are in restricted territory, and you were supposed to stop and show us your I.D. and Pass. We have strict orders for anyone that does not do this to shoot them right then and there on the spot. But I can't—you're nuns. How can I shoot nuns?"

It was then that the realization hit me why he was so upset: I was inside the Air Force Base! Because of my fixation on the plane, I had gone through without even noticing that I took the wrong divided road.

With him still yelling over and over again, "You are nuns – I just can't shoot nuns," all I wanted to do was to get out of there as fast I could. So I just yelled back to the young soldier, "I'm terribly sorry—I took the wrong road." And with that, I hurried and turned the car around and got out of there. As we were leaving, I looked out the rear-view mirror—and the poor young man was just standing there like a statue, looking at us.

By some unforeseen miracle, the Aunt made it to the plane just before it took off. Relieved that she was on the plane, I turned to go back home—and believe me, when we came to the divide in the road, I drove the car as fast as I could past that part of the divide. All I wanted to do was to get out of there and go home.

HOSPITALS AND SICKNESS
Tale # 1: The Outrageous Hospital Bill

Part of our outreach as Sisters, was to visit the Nursing Homes and Hospitals. We would first ask the patients if they would like us to visit with them for a couple of minutes, and usually we were always welcomed to do so. However, we would respect their wishes if they didn't want us to visit with them. And we would not impose by praying or speaking to them of anything religious, unless they themselves brought it up first or asked us to do so. Hopefully, we were there just to make them to feel just a little bit better by our presence.

This one time when I was in the hospital, I was visiting with an elderly patient. He seemed so very upset, so I asked if there was anything I could do to help him. He replied, "I'm upset because I am going home today, and I just read my hospital bill. It is terribly high. It's an outrage, all of the things they are charging me for—and worst of all, they are even charging me for going to the bathroom."

I looked at him, wondering if he wasn't thinking clearly, most likely due to his medication. Or could it possibly be that they *did* include that in his bill? As I had never been in the hospital, myself, in twenty-some years, I didn't really have a clue about how much and for what they charged, any more. So I said to him, "You know, I'm sure that they wouldn't be charging you for using the bathroom."

"Oh yes they did," he replied.

I asked again, "Are you really sure that they charged for using the bathroom?"

Giving me a disgusted look and showing his irritation with me for not believing him, he replied, "Yes, they did. Just look at this bill, it is right here in this bill. You just take a good look at it and you will see that I am right – they *do* charge me for using the bathroom."

I took the bill from him and started reading it. When I got to the middle, I saw what he was talking about. What he thought was the *lav*atory actually was the *labor*atory.

Tale # 2: Only In the Eyes of a Child

Another time when I was visiting the hospital as a nun, at that time I was wearing the Habit that fully covered your body—and I mean, covered your body. Our heads were completely covered, as well, by what we called a "headgear."

Part of the headgear was a white material, just like a white pillowcase except that it had an opening for our face to show through; and the bottom part covered our shoulders, with white folds going across our chest. A stiff white band was tied around our forehead; and the purpose of this very stiff white band was to hold up the black veil that covered the top of our head and went down the back of our heads.

I'm sure you are wondering why I am being so descriptive about the headgear. It's because it is very important for the telling of this short tale.

I was walking down the hallway of the Hospital, and I noticed that a little boy was staring at me. I could tell by his face that he had never seen a nun dressed like me, before. As I kept walking toward the little boy, he was still looking at me. I couldn't tell by his face why he was staring at me the way he was. Could it be that he was afraid of me, since he was alone? In fact, we were the only two people in the hallway at that time.

When I got close, I decided to go over to him and let him know that he needn't be afraid of me. As I did so, he yelled out in a very loud voice—I'm sure everyone in all the rooms could hear him yell—"Lady, what kind of an accident were you in???"

Tale # 3: Bronchitis and Me

When I was a nun in my thirties, I lived in a small town in Oregon. It was in 1968 and I had come down with the Hong Kong flu. Actually, I'm not certain that it was this flu. All I am sure of is that I came down with a bad flu, and from it I developed bronchitis. It was so bad that for a full month, every day I would go to the hospital, and they would give me a shot in my behind that smelled like camphor or Mentholatum. The shot hurt so badly that I felt like I had been kicked by a mule. (Mind you, I never *have* been kicked by a mule, but I bet anything that it would have been just the same as that shot they would give me in the hospital.) Then they would lay me on a hospital table and put a heavy woolen blanket on my chest, and on top of this blanket on my chest they would place a large metal-type lid that had heat in it, and I would stay there for 20 minutes every day.

From that day on, I was told to be very careful and try to keep from getting colds, etc.

In the month of June, after school was out I would go and teach summer school for two weeks in another Parish in another town. When my doctor heard that I would be teaching summer school, and from there going on to Oregon State University to take classes there for the rest of the summer, he told me that I had to be very careful not to catch cold. And if it looked like I was going to catch cold, then I would have to go to a doctor with a prescription for a shot (the same one I was given in the hospital), and so he wrote out a prescription to take with me in case I needed to have this shot.

It was a more than five-hour trip to get to where I was to teach summer school, three hundred miles away. I would stay at the Rectory, where the Irish Priest lived with his mother from Ireland who kept house and cooked for her son.

The second week I was there, I woke up in the morning and could feel my throat being a little sore, so I knew that it was the beginning of a cold. I told the Priest that I needed to go to the doctor and explained to him the reason why. So he called his own personal doctor for an appointment. Then he drove me to the doctor's office, and he himself stayed out in the car to wait for me.

I went in and gave the doctor the prescription that my own doctor had given me. Well, let me tell you, I don't know if this doctor read the prescription right or not but not only did I feel like I got kicked in the back end by *two* donkeys instead of just one, but the prescription was so very strong that it permeated every part of me, I kid you not. I could even taste it in my mouth, and it tasted horrible! It was like I ate a mothball (though I never actually have done so), and it permeated my body all over and made me feel like I smelled like one huge mothball walking around.

I left the doctor's office and got in the car where the Priest was waiting for me. I wondered if he could smell me, as I felt that I was reeking from the shot. But all the way back, he never mentioned anything, and he acted as if he didn't smell me. Not knowing him, and this being my first time teaching for him, I felt relieved that he had not noticed anything. When we got to the Rectory and I got out of his car and went indoors from the garage, he took hold of my hand.

I really took exception to this, and I said to him in an upset voice, "What are you doing?"

"Never mind," he said to me, still holding my hand with such a grip that I could not pull it loose, "just follow me"—all the time holding my hand. He then took me into the parlor; the office; his bedroom; the living room where he and his mom spent the evenings together; and then into the dining room. I was thinking to myself, *What kind of a nut is he? He's not all there – he must have a screw loose in his brain, somewhere.* With him still holding my hand, we went into the kitchen, where his mother was preparing the noon meal. And as he let go of my hand, he said to her, "Well, mom, we won't have to worry about any moths or bugs in our home, as we have it well fumigated!" Yes, he had smelled me!

Tale # 4: The Best Medicine Ever!

About a year later, this same Priest was visiting the Pastor whom we were working for, and our Pastor happened to tell him that I had been quite sick with a very bad cold and that it didn't help my bronchial condition, either. So this Priest, now knowing me from my teaching in his Parish, came over to the Convent and asked for me.

I went into the parlor, and there he was, standing and holding a huge bottle of whiskey. (In fact, I still have not seen a bottle that large, even to this day.) He handed me the bottle and said to me, "Here, Sister, take a shot of this every night before you go to bed. If it doesn't kill the bug, it will at least keep him happy."

End of Story – Amen!

THE TOWN SCROOGE

In the town where we Sisters were stationed, there was a man who owned several properties, so he was not poor by any means. However, he lived in a shack, and was not the friendliest of persons. Sad to say, the poor man did not have any friends or family, to my knowledge, and he never seemed to smile when you would see him.

I felt very sorry for him, and I would stop to talk with him when I saw him on the streets. And although he seemed gruff and annoyed that I was talking with him, yet at the same time I knew he was enjoying our wee chat together. I would ask him how he was feeling, and in response I would get a long series of all his troubles, and that he was not long for this world. I, in turn, would show sympathy for him, which he acted gruff about; and yet when I looked in his eyes, I could see he was touched that I cared. I would get a kick out of him when I was out on the street and he would be maybe several blocks away and I could see him walking just as natural as me – but when he would suddenly see me, then all of a sudden he would be bent over, wobbling and looking like it was all he could do to stand on his two feet, and would give the impression that he was very ill and weak.

As time went on, however, he actually he did end up in the hospital. The Parish Priest and we Sisters would go and visit him there, and bring him little treats. When it came time for him

to come home, the administrator of the hospital was most concerned, as it was time for this man to leave the hospital but he
had no one whosoever to care for him, which he would need until he was fully recuperated.

Our Priest, Father Ambrose, offered to have him come
and stay with him, and he would care for this elderly man. And
that is just what happened. This one evening, Father Ambrose,
who did his own cooking, invited Sister and me to have supper
with him and the elderly man. I was so enjoying my meal, as
Father was a very good cook; when all of a sudden, the elderly
man took out his false teeth and right at the table, he started
cleaning off the food that had gotten attached to them. Needless
to say, my appetite was gone, and so ended my supper. And on
that, I will end this story.

A SERIES OF MIXED TALES

Tale # 1: I'm Always Happy to Do a Favor

In another town where I was stationed in 1972, there were two very nice young men who lived right next door to our Convent. I would often stop and chat with them if they happened to be outside in their yard. This one summer, as I was chatting with them, they told me that they were going away on vacation for a week, and would I mind watering the garden in the back of their house twice a day for them while they were gone—once in the morning, and again in the evening just before the sun went down. Feeling happy that I had a chance to do a good deed for them, I quickly said that yes, I would be glad to water the garden for them.

They left for their vacation, and I faithfully watered the beautiful, lush green plants that were growing in rows, filling almost all of their small backyard. And as I watered them, I kept wondering what kind of a leafy vegetable I was watering, as I had never seen any vegetable plant look like that before. I just couldn't help but be in awe of how beautiful they were, and I thought that just maybe these neighbors would share with us whatever it was that I was watering.

When they came back from their vacation, they thanked me profusely for doing such a great job in keeping their garden watered, and that it couldn't have looked better. It just made me so proud and happy that they were so pleased with my watering.

Still, I thought it was strange that they never offered any of the produce from the plants I had so faithfully watered, morning and night, as a thank-you for doing such a good job.

I really cannot remember how long it was after I had watered the garden for the two men that I happened to be looking out of the Convent window. And to my astonishment, I saw a police car out in front of their house—and both of them, with handcuffs on, being put inside the police car. I couldn't imagine what was going on—what did they do to get arrested? They seemed to be such lovely, kind men—should I run out and find out what was going on? But then I had second thoughts and decided to stay put at the window until the police car drove away.

Later that week, the mystery of the arrest was solved for me. It was then that I found out that what I was watering were not lush, leafy green vegetables, but marijuana. End of Story! Amen! Amen!

Tale # 2: "Isn't Sister Good to You?"

In New York in the 1950s and '60s, Religion classes were part of the curriculum in the public school system. Religion classes would be taught during the regular school time, on different days of the week. Tests were given and graded in the upper grades, from 7th through the 12th, as part of the public school curriculum.

When it came time for me to teach, I would stand at the door of my classroom and wait for all the kids to arrive. As I would be standing there, I could hear the Irish Sister across the hall from me saying over and over again to the first-graders in her class, "Now, isn't Sister good to you?" and the response from each child would be, "Yes, Sister, thank you, Sister." One day, curiosity got the better of me. And while waiting for the rest of my class to arrive, and hearing the repetitive, "Isn't Sister good to you?" coming from across the hall, I decided go over to the Irish Sister's classroom and peek in to find out what was going on.

I found out. Here was the Sister going from one child to the other and placing one Jelly Bean candy on their desk—and at the same time she was doing it, she would say, "Now, isn't Sister good to you?"

Tale # 3: Oh, What Happened?

In the Catholic Church has what is called Confession, where Catholics go to confess their sins to the Priest and ask for forgiveness. Before our children receive First Communion, they have what we call Making Their First Confession.

I was in charge of preparing the young children for their first Confession. Our Pastor was very strict and expected everything to be just right; and if it wasn't, he would severely chastise the children, verbally. Knowing this, I went over and over with children what they were to say in the Confessional as part of confessing their sins, as I did not want the Pastor to get after them. When the day came, I was so nervous as I watched them go into the Confessional room one by one, as I didn't want them to make any mistakes. (To be honest, I always felt that these little ones were too young to really sin—maybe they did misdeeds, but not sin –yet it was the tradition of the Church, so it had to be done.)

When they were through confessing their sins, the children would go up to the front of the Church and say the penance for their sins that the Priest would give them. The penance would be prayers; it could be one prayer, or saying the prayer more times than once. And that was the penance.

I just happened to look at the children kneeling and saying their penance, when I noticed at little girl just sobbing like everything. My heart went down to my feet, so to speak. *Oh my,*

I thought to myself, *what happened in the Confessional? Father must have gotten after her. Oh, the poor little one.* I went up to where she was kneeling, and I looked at her sad face with tears streaming down from her eyes. I hurried to put one arm around her, and was drying her tears with the other hand and at the same time saying to her, "My dear, what happened – what's wrong?"

Sobbing, she said to me, "Father gave me *two* 'Our Fathers' to say, and I know only *one*." End of Story.

Tale # 4: The State Catholic Conference for Women: Their Role in the Church

Don't ask me why, but even to this day I am not really certain why I was picked to give the main presentation and talk on the subject of "The Role of Women in the Church" at the conference, as I felt there were many qualified women besides me. However, I was, and so I have a story to share with you.

At this particular conference, not only were the women and Catholic Sisters present, but there were Priests and the Bishop there as well. After I had finished my presentation, I opened up a chance for questions or comments. At the end of the discussion, one woman put up her hand for me to call on her, which I did; and she had this question for me: "Sister, when you enter the classroom, do you make your students stand up as you come in?" I promptly replied, "No, I do not. The reason is that I feel respect cannot be demanded—respect is something you must earn. So therefore I do not require my students to stand up upon entering a room." This being the last question, I sat back down on my chair on the podium.

It was now the Bishop's turn to speak. The protocol is that you always stand up for the Bishop—not only when he enters a room, but when he gets up to speak as well. (This was back in the 1970s, and I don't know if this is still required of the laity, today.) As the Bishop was getting up from his chair to speak, after my speech on showing respect where I said, "Respect is something you earn and can't demand," all the people in the room didn't know whether to remain sitting or to stand up.

If you are a baseball fan or know about the game, then you will be familiar with the WAVE. Section by section in the stands where people are seated will, by cue, stand up and immediately sit down; and then the other section follows suit; and it goes on and on. Well, that is how it looked among those in the audience. Some who were sitting got up to stand and then quickly sat down, and then others would stand and then sit down. When the Bishop reached the podium and saw the spectacle in front of him, with his face turning red, he motioned for everyone to sit down. I often wonder if I might not have set a new precedent of not standing for religious dignitaries in the Diocese of Wyoming.

So with this last Tale, I will now bring my book of Tales to an end.

PART XI

EPILOGUE

In 1978, after twenty-seven years in the Community of Sisters, I left the Convent.

I did so because the Community that I belonged to was going to return to the old way of Convent life—the way it was before Pope John the Twenty-Third came along and had the sisters update their lifestyle. Knowing that I could not go back to the old way of living, after a year of prayer and much pondering over the decision that I would have to make, I decided to leave the Convent, and thus asked to be released from my Vows.

Since I was qualified in Social Service Work and Counseling, I had planned on working in this area, and so put in resumes to that effect. However, two different employment agencies gave me interviews with churches; so from that, I understood that this was where God still wanted me to be. And the best part of it all was that in doing so, I was able to also carry on the work that I did as a Sister in the Convent—Counseling and Social Service Work—which brought a heightened feeling of satisfaction and fulfillment into my life.

Seven years after leaving the Convent, I married the Love of My Life. We were together for twenty-three years before my dear husband, Sean, passed away in 2008 of the Brain Cancer that he had been diagnosed with thirteen years earlier in our married life.

My wish for you is that you will always have the Gift of Laughter to help carry you through your journey in life; and if you had at least one good laugh or one smile, or even enjoyed a little escapism in reading my Tales, then I have fulfilled my mission and desire in writing this book.

I would like to conclude by leaving you with an Irish Blessing, taken from—of all places—a magnet on my refrigerator door (which is next to another magnet on my refrigerator door that reads: "Thou Shalt Not Weigh More Than Thy Refrigerator"):

AN IRISH BLESSING

May you have a song in your heart,

A smile on your lips,

And nothing but joy at your fingertips.

ABOUT THE AUTHOR

As this entire book is "about the author," the only other thing to say about Eloise Aitken Farren is that she is still a very active, vibrant woman who still loves to come in contact with, and enjoys relating to, all people of different backgrounds, races, lifestyles, and beliefs—religious believers and non-believers, and those with different views. Having these associations has so enriched her life that she calls this her "Banquet of Life." Her personal philosophy is that every person she meets and associates with is important to her and worthy of unconditional love and respect.

Oh yes—she still loves to tell stories and make people laugh. And if she can help lighten someone's life, even if only for minute, then she knows that she is fulfilling her purpose in living.

CPSIA information can be obtained
at www.ICGtesting.com
Printed in the USA
FSOW02n1039280417
33519FS

9 780981 627854